RAY OLDENBURG

Celebrating the Third Place

Ray Oldenburg, Ph.D.,
professor emeritus of sociology
at the University of West Florida,
coined the term "third place" and is
widely recognized as one of the world's
leading advocates for great good places. His
book, *The Great Good Place*, a *New York Times Book
Review* Editor's Choice for 1989, was reissued
in 1999. He is frequently sought after as a
media commentator and consultant to
entrepreneurs and community and
urban planners. He lives in
Pensacola, Florida.

EDITED AND WITH AN INTRODUCTION BY
RAY OLDENBURG

Celebrating the Third Place

Inspiring Stories about the
"Great Good Places"
at the Heart of Our
Communities

MARLOWE & COMPANY
NEW YORK

Published by
Marlowe & Company
An Imprint of Avalon Publishing Group Incorporated
161 William Street, 16th Floor
New York, NY 10038

Library of Congress Cataloging-in-Publication Data is available.
ISBN 1-56924-612-2

9   8   7   6   5   4   3   2   1

Designed by Pauline Neuwirth, Neuwirth & Associates, Inc.

Printed in the United States of America
Distributed by Publishers Group West

to Roberta Brandes Gratz

Contents

CONTENTS

Celebrating the Third Place

Introduction

$\mathcal{A}$ **young lady's** father sits at the big round table in the little diner taking his morning coffee just as he has almost every day for the past ten years. His friends are there with him. His daughter thinks it's a wonderful place and was moved to tell me about it in writing. Among the many goings-on she described, the following best illustrates the reason for her admiration:

> During my senior year, our band had been chosen to march in the Rose Bowl Parade. A friend of mine who was also a band member could not afford the nine hundred dollars required to make the trip. He was from a broken home, and was forced to live in a taxicab for three years and watch his mom snort cocaine. Having done drugs since the age of ten, this seventeen-year-old recovered addict presented an amazing story. He cleaned himself up on his own, and moved into the home of a drug counselor at school. He began going to church, participating in extracurricular activities, and tried to make up the academics he had avoided for so long. The drug counselor's home was average-sized, but housed a family of six. There was barely room for my friend and absolutely no money. He slept on three couch cushions, which was a luxury compared to the taxi. With all the help this family had provided for him, there was just no way they could afford to finance his band trip. I expressed my concern to my

father. The following morning, he spoke to his all-male coffee group about my friend. It only took a quarter of an hour to convince them. One pulled out a hundred-dollar bill and laid it on the table. Several followed his lead, laying hundreds, fifties, and twenties out on the round table. Within just a few minutes, there lay nine hundred dollars. My dad went to the school and deposited the money into my friend's account. No one ever knew where the money came from. That's the way they wanted it.

It is the kind of thing Tocqueville marveled at when he visited America in the 1830s, the capacity of Americans to do what needs doing without depending upon government. Essential to informal collective effort is the habit of association, and essential to informal association are places where people may gather freely and frequently and with relative ease.

That little diner is just such a place. It is what I call a "third place," a setting beyond home and work (the "first" and "second" places respectively) in which people relax in good company and do so on a regular basis. Many Americans, though not nearly enough, still give allegiance to a place they visit before or after work and when home life permits. Some have coffee there before work. Some have a beer there after work. Some stop in for the Luncheon Special every Thursday. Some drop by whenever it's convenient. It is their version of the once popular television series *Cheers*.

Such association is not as essential for good works as it once was. Our society, alas, has become much like Tocqueville's homeland, in which governmental agencies are expected to do whatever needs doing. Yet what government does is done remotely and impersonally; its focus is on our weaknesses and dependencies and its policies define us accordingly.

We may not need third place association to build a town hall anymore, but we sorely need it to construct the infrastructures of human relationships. Ever since the solidifying effect of World War II passed into history, Americans have been growing further apart from one another. Lifestyles are increasingly privatized and competitive; residential areas are increasingly devoid of gathering places. To the extent of our affluence, we avoid public parks, public playgrounds, public schools, and public transportation.

Awareness of these trends and of the sharp decline in the number of third places in the United States prompted me to write *The Great Good Place* a decade ago. That volume details, illustrates, and analyzes informal public gathering places both here and abroad. It identifies their many social functions and their unique importance as focal points of community life. Now in its third edition, *The Great Good Place* has become basic reading among a growing number of groups encouraging revitalization of our urban areas and of public life.

That book and the publicity it received also brought me into contact with many people who own and operate third places or otherwise have intimate knowledge of them. It became obvious to me that these people have stories to tell that can take our understanding well beyond what I offered in the first book. It remained only to contact them requesting their participation.

Contributors were given free rein as to style, length, and format in the hope that these latitudes would allow them to bring their places to life in these pages. And so they have. Much, I think, will be accomplished by their efforts. There is a lot of how-to in these chapters and much that is inspirational. Some will find resolve to open a place or to remodel with a third place vision in mind. Still more will resolve to find a third place and the human connection it brings.

The collection as a whole should broaden the reader's view of new possibilities for third place association. Earlier versions have faded, such as candy stores, soda fountains, gun shops, and male taverns. Coffeehouses and health spas are on the rise, but other versions are needed.

Importantly, these accounts will give the reader a fine sense of what constitutes the *real thing*. Developers build houses and call them "homes." They build socially sterile subdivisions and call them "communities." It's called "warming the product." It's also happening with alleged third places. Officials of a popular coffeehouse chain often claim that their establishments are third places, but they aren't. They may evolve into them but at present, they are high volume, fast turnover operations that present an institutional ambience at an intimate level. Seating is uncomfortable by design and customers in line are treated rudely when uncertain of their orders.

Visiting Celebration, Florida, my wife and I arrived at its version of a friendly diner three minutes late for breakfast and were told it couldn't be served. "Three minutes," I protested, "Are you certain we can't have breakfast?" The man was quite certain. To my wife's embarrassment, we left to find breakfast elsewhere. The "friendly diner" struck me as much a fake as the "Town Hall" across the street. The Disney people have their policies and small towns have their ways and ne'er the twain shall meet.

A popular restaurant chain locates its establishments along the more congested commercial strips but nonetheless insists that they are your "neighborhood" restaurants. Other restaurants, sometimes even in neon, claim to be "gathering places." As Bruce Katz and Jennifer Bradley recently noted, "People are honestly trying to balance the frantic privacy of the suburbs with some kind of spontaneous public life."[1] One may expect to see increased pandering to this need with the result that third places may be marketed but not delivered.

THIRD PLACE AS A VICTORY

Victories are achieved as the result of a struggle against the odds and the odds have been increasingly stacked against third places since the end of World War II. The best third places are locally owned, independent, small-scale, steady-state business, and both government and incorporated chain operations have wreaked havoc upon them.

It is no coincidence that chains and unifunctional zoning emerged in tandem. Unifunctional zoning prohibits commercial establishments in residential areas such that Americans "have to get into the car for everything" and when they do, they drive to strips and malls where only the chains can afford to lease. Before unifunctional or negative zoning dictated land use, little stores, taverns, offices, and eateries were located within walking distance of most town and city dwellers and those places constituted "the stuff of community."

---

1. Katz, Bruce and Bradley, Jennifer. "Divided We Sprawl," The Atlantic Monthly (December 1999): 42.

Those small businesses typically drew most of their trade from within a two- or three-block radius and survived quite nicely. The chain operations could not have competed with them on their own terms. A "McBurger" on every block would not produce the volume and turnover such establishments require in order to flourish. Negative zoning thus set the stage such that these cloned and impersonal chains thrived, and they did so by killing off the independents.

The personnel and the policies that the chains bring to town are a far cry from what local independents offered. Many of the people who operated the mom-and-pop stores were "public characters," as Jane Jacobs called them—people who knew everyone in the neighborhood and cared about them. Those folks kept an eye on the children, kept an eye on the neighborhood, and kept people informed on matters of mutual concern. In contrast, chain personnel turnover is high and "wasting time" with customers is discouraged. No matter how bad the weather, letting people in before the appointed minute is just as unthinkable as adjusting the menu to local tastes.

Successful third places are also harder to achieve because several decades of poor urban planning have encouraged people to stay at home. "Nesting" or "cocooning" are reported to be favored by increasing numbers of Americans. As the public sphere became more inhospitable and enervating to get around in, the private sphere improved. Homes are better equipped, more comfortable, and more entertaining than ever before. This domestic retreat presents a challenge to Traditional Town Planning or the New Urbanism, which purports to restore community and public life by offering a proven alternative to the anti-community tract housing that spread like a plague after World War II.

The New Urbanism incorporates principles of architecture and layout similar to those developed in the 1920s when we knew how to build communities and proceeded accordingly. But is the architectural remedy sufficient?

In a recent feature in Preservation Magazine, Alan Ehrenhalt focuses on a public square well located and designed to attract the townspeople—but it doesn't.[2] His account reminded me of an automobile trip I took a

2. Ehrenhalt, Alan. "The Empty Square," *Preservation Magazine* (March/April 2000): 42–51.

few years ago, during which I made stops at the Clock Tower Square in Marion, Illinois, "The Hill" in St. Louis, the town square in Bloomfield, Iowa, and a little town-within-a-town in East Superior, Wisconsin. All were the kinds of settings idealized in New Urbanist planning. All were visited during those first warm days of spring that used to draw people out like bears from hibernation. All of them, unfortunately, were also suitable places for rifle practice. Nobody was out and about.

The strong suggestion is that it will take more than front porches, reduced setbacks, and mixed use planning to re-create public life. Front porch use was popular before television and air-conditioning, but has not been popular since. And people have become even more reclusive since universal ownership of computers has become national policy.

I spoke with a man the other day who regularly walks his dogs around an expansive residential circle. Lately, he's been seeing fewer of his neighbors and began asking what's happened to them. The answer usually is that they're on the Net, some playing the market, some in chat rooms, some spending countless hours playing FreeCell or solitaire.

This is not to suggest, however, that people won't come out. It is to suggest that towns and cities that want life on the streets and a community spirit to prevail will have to take steps to promote it.

A good example is that of Harrisburg, Pennsylvania, which suffered years of economic stagnation and a devastating storm, and for which revitalization took concerted effort. Shortly before Harrisburg made its comeback, I gave a public lecture at the North Street Café and Trading Center and was informed that that third place had recently opened and had been given an award by Mayor Reed for contributing to the betterment of the city.

It was not the way city hall usually treats independent, start-up businesses. Typically, a parade of inspectors is better at harassing than helping, and if the business is successful there are not likely to be any official thank-you's.

I have no doubt that the mayor's hospitality toward new business reverberated in the hospitality the city now offers to all who live or visit there. Always a walkable city, its public sphere is now great fun to enter. Young Jim Maturani and Michael DeFazio, who opened on North Street, have since been joined by many others who bid welcome to those "on the town" or just seeking respite from daily routines. This medium-sized city hosts a public life that larger centers may well envy.

Harrisburg's architecture confirms New Urbanist thinking and it was protected in the same manner as the French Quarter in New Orleans. Economic stagnation discouraged corporate expansionism and urban renewal, thus preserving an urban landscape built to human scale and made interesting by a fine-grained pattern of mixed land use. Its seventeen-square-mile downtown remains walkable and charming and all the more interesting lately because there are people around in numbers not seen in years. Harrisburg illustrates the dual need for an inviting physical setting and the efforts of people who know how to implement hospitality.

As a final comment on the victorious character of successful third places in America today, I remind the reader that we personally experience the difficulty in the loss of our free hour. Working adults formerly enjoyed an hour of "community time" after the workday was over and before they were expected home. It has been replaced by an hour of "commuting time." The former warmed us to our fellow human beings, the latter conditions us to hate them.

Why did we lose our free hour? It all had to do with planners who focused on cars and their movement and forgot about people and how they live. Unlike European autobahns, our interstate highways were routed right through our cities such that local travelers found the roads congested by people who didn't even want to be in town. Street systems were designed in such a way that most roads carry too little traffic while others carry too much. Unifunctional zoning encouraged urban sprawl such that not only do Americans have to drive everywhere they go but, their necessary destinations are farther away from home than are those of peoples in other countries are from their homes. Finally, the auto industry managed to kill the trolley systems and put forty vehicles on the road in place of the one vehicle that carried the same number of passengers. Road rage may be understandable, but it is directed at the wrong people.

It is no longer easy to establish a good third place, but those who manage to do so are, to that extent, all the more heroic in their efforts to hold on to community for the rest of us. This book is theirs and they speak to us from where they live and from what they hold dear in life.

Students build composting bins at Annie's Gift and Garden Shop.

Annie's Gift and Garden Shop

AMHERST, MASSACHUSETTS

MOST THIRD places enjoy a location where pedestrian traffic is heavy and many regulars live but minutes away. Annie's, however, is located out in the rural countryside and the reader will learn how she cleverly lures people into her place and quickly convinces them that she is interested in much more than making money.

Raised in a small tobacco town in the South, Annie was deeply influenced by a small restaurant that served as the local gathering place. It was one of those wonderful spots in which "everybody knows your name" and cares about you. That little restaurant, Fred's Place, embodied her dream of what to offer the public, even though her plant nursery differs sharply in both its offerings and location.

Like Lynne Breaux, whose story also appears in this collection, Annie Cheatham is a woman steeped in the traditions of southern hospitality and determined to bring it north. She has succeeded famously.

In the spring of my sophomore year at St. Mary's College, I got pneumonia. St. Mary's is a small Episcopal women's college in Raleigh, North Carolina, and in 1961 the infirmary occupied an old house on the campus. Two nurses staffed the facility, and I was the only patient. I was unhappy there, didn't get well, and after a week my parents took me home to the hospital. The doctor ordered glucose and antibiotics, and as soon as I was well enough to eat solid food, my parents asked what I wanted. "A hot dog from Fred's," I said. That night the second floor hall of the Johnston County Memorial Hospital reeked of Fred Adams' chili sauce, and I was one meal closer to recovery.

Fred's Place was a small restaurant on Third Street next door to Creech's Drugstore and Stallings' Jewelry in Smithfield, a rural tobacco town. Fred's was narrow and long, about fifteen by forty feet. It was poorly lit. A long bar stretched the length of the room. Small café tables lined the left wall. Fred worked alone behind the bar on the right.

Fred served hot dogs, sodas in glass bottles, potato chips, and fried pork rinds. He only bought quality wieners and steamed the buns until they were spongy and soft. His mustard and relish were spicy, but the chili sauce was what made his hot dogs special. It had ground beef in it, chili pepper, and tomato sauce—common ingredients in any cookbook recipe. But it had something else, a secret from Fred, and I never found out what that was. It was the best chili I have ever eaten on a hot dog.

Everybody ate at Fred's at one time or another. Lawyers in suits arguing cases at the county courthouse slipped into Fred's during the court's lunchtime recess. Tobacco farmers in stained overalls ate at Fred's. My father picked up a Fred's hot dog whenever Creech's called with a prescription or just before having his hair cut at the barbershop on the corner. In the hospital with pneumonia, I wanted a Fred's hot dog because Fred's meant home.

Bernice's Beauty Parlor, Talton's Grocery, the Fashion Shop, and other public places in my hometown of four thousand also meant home. They not only provided services we needed, they also provided a sense of community. Adults in these places knew me and they cared about me, not in an overbearing or intrusive way, but enough so I noticed. I wasn't invisible. I had a name and people used it, sometimes to steer me back in the right direction. I've always been grateful for being known in that way. I liked the intimacy, and ever since then, I've looked for places that offer that kind of arm's-length caring. I rarely find it. When I started Annie's Garden and Gift Store, I was determined to create it.

I had to face the differences. Annie's is not Fred's or Creech's, and Amherst, Massachusetts is not Smithfield. Annie's is not even located in a downtown. The store sits on a six-acre parcel on a major state road, Route 116, at the edge of Amherst township. Small agricultural enterprises surround it—a fish farm, organic vegetable farm, and another, part-time, farmer who raises a dozen cattle a year. Annie's uses two acres of the six;

clover is planted on the rest and the cattle farmer cuts and bales it in June and October.

It is no longer the late 1940s and 1950s and Annie's is not located in the rural South. Our customers are New Englanders, as friendly as southerners once you get to know them, but more reserved and reticent at first. They live in small communities scattered up and down the Connecticut River, each with its own town center. People are busier now than they were when I was growing up, and our customers don't have the leisure time that my parents' generation had.

But Annie's did not emerge from a vacuum. And those early experiences in Smithfield informed me as I envisioned my new business. My business would be a place, like Fred's, where people would be known. That is what I remembered about my hometown; that is what I longed for myself. But it would be more than that. Because I am a teacher, it would be a place where people learned, became more competent and proficient. Because I am a student of religions and spirituality, it would be a place of beauty and rest, a sacred place in a busy world. Because I am a writer, it would be a place that plays with words. And because I believe in and practice organic gardening, it would be a place where a healthy connection between gardens and nature would be evident.

Our first challenge was to attract customers and make sales. I opened in 1992 when the New England economy was deep in a recession. Businesses were closing, not opening; banks were calling in loans, not making them; and employees were leaving the area for the South and the West. But like every entrepreneur who's ever started a business, I was convinced that I had a good idea and that I could beat the odds and make it work. I knew organic gardening; I knew people loved gardening; I knew how to make beautiful places; and I guessed that others were just as hungry for places like Fred's as I was. Surely we could put together a combination that would succeed.

Drivers on Route 116 were our most obvious market. The road is heavily traveled, but our building is not part of a strip mall. The only reason for anybody to stop at Annie's is because we have something they want. From the start we knew we would have to grab the drivers going by who were on their way to someplace else. We knew that we cared about them, wanted to know them, and that we had something special to offer them, but we had to get them in the door before they would know that.

Every dime we had was going into restoring the dilapidated building and landscaping the grounds, but I knew that I'd have to spend money on a sign board with large changeable letters if we wanted to communicate with the drivers passing by. A few weeks before opening, we took the plunge, ordered an expensive set of letters and hung the board. We started by wrapping our messages around the sign—one phrase on the south side, the punch line on the north. "Only fourteen more days to open," we'd say on one side. On the other, "Honk if you think we'll make it." We kept this theme until we opened. "Ever start a business?/Come in and tell us how." "What's the secret to success?/Details, Details, Details." "Only five more days to open/Miracles do happen." "Grand Opening Today/Whew, We made it!" On opening day, smiling people came in to investigate, and we were in business.

Since that day, our sign has taken on significance for members of our whole community. We respond to requests for birthdays, graduations, anniversaries, and memorials. We read local papers and congratulate award winners. These strangers may or may not be customers, may or may not drive down Route 116 that day. But someone will see the sign and call the honoree, and by day's end, a bunch of people will be out there taking pictures and posing.

We use the sign to make fun of ourselves and our products. "Annie told me to change the sign/So I did." "Too hot, closed early/Gone swimming." "Trees marked to move/Help pay for our vacation." Faith Deering, a regular customer, recently recalled one of her favorite sign stories. "My son Dan and I were driving home one evening. Both of us were tired and cranky and neither of us was communicative. When we got to Annie's store, we both craned our necks to read the message, and it said, 'Come in/Tell me what to have for supper.' Dan responds positively to calls for help and he loves cooking, so he immediately said, 'Pull in, Mama, and I'll tell her what to cook!' After a good conversation with Annie, we left feeling far cheerier and full of ideas for our own family suppers. I have often wondered how many people's moods have been shifted or attitudes changed by a few words on that sign."

We are also reflective and philosophical on our sign. "What is profit?/Top soil, leaf mold, compost." "Breathe/Keep breathing." "Do you have the answer?/What is the question?" And we play with the national news. After Monica Lewinsky turned in her stained blue dress and incriminated President Bill Clinton in a sex scandal, we put all blue flowers on sale. After a state of the union message, we wrote, "My fellow Americans/What is the state of your union?" During the Senate hearings and vote for Supreme Court Justice Clarence Thomas, we took a stand: "I believe Anita Hill."

We tackle local news. In the spring of 1996, an adult pornography shop opened in a nearby town and the owner put a two-foot-wide banner across the front of his store saying, "Topless Coming Soon." He got a lot of media attention and offended many people, but nobody could stop him. We decided to have some fun with the story, and on our sign we wrote, "Topless birdbaths/Topless statuary." A local paper ran a story about our spoof; customers came in laughing, and bought a few things, the tops and bottoms of birdbaths.

We communicate with drivers with other signs as well. A sign across our one-acre field reads, "Annie's Employees' Fitness Center," a spoof on other local businesses that build gymnasiums for desk-bound workers. And every November when darkness begins to lengthen on our New England days, we write "Light Comes" with lights on the side of our building to signify the coming of the solstice and the turning toward spring. We keep it lit until early March. Faith Deering reflected on what this sign meant to her when she first saw it. "In the early darkness of January evenings, 'Light Comes' caught my eye. It was reassuring and hopeful, a beacon I looked forward to on my daily drive from Amherst to home. As the winter wore on, I became intrigued and wondered about the creator of the sign. The store was closed for the season"—We used to close for the winter months; now we are a year-round business—"so I left a message in the mailbox expressing the pleasure I got from the words."

Annie's signs are community bulletin board, political soapbox, Zen center, pun-of-the-week poster, and awards banquet rolled into one. With them we nag, brag, love and adore, call names, point fingers, weep, and pray. In an age of information overload, our signs demonstrate an intelligence inside the business, a wit, a political and spiritual consciousness. "Somebody is thinking in there," our passersby might say.

Once people come into Annie's, they quickly find that they are our first priority. We want to know our customers. We lean across the counter and ask about vacations and school activities, illness and recoveries, births and deaths. Because of our southern hospitality, our warmth and openness, our customers reveal themselves to us. One customer called the day she learned she had cancer to order an indoor fountain; another cried as she described a grave site where she wanted to plant bulbs; another came to tell us his first child had been born the night before; another to introduce us to his three sons on Father's Day. Paola Di Stefano explained how Annie's staff responds when she comes in. "I'm always greeted warmly and by name, and the staff's desire to help me and answer my questions goes way beyond what I'd expect of any store. They have loaned me tools, called me with information that I had requested, inquired about my garden, my health, a tool I'd bought several years earlier, and garden fantasies that I'd shared but never expected to put into practice. It feels as though they have a memory of *me*."

Whenever you go to a place where people know and like you, you open yourself to others who are there. This happens at Annie's all the time. Customers run into people they know and pass information back and forth. Regular customers answer questions of new gardeners when our staff can't answer them. Often we see people exchanging phone numbers or business cards. For several years, Faith Deering, an entomologist, displayed an educational exhibit about monarch butterflies—five or six chrysalises in a jar and a flyer about the life cycle of monarchs. We all got caught up in the drama of the emergence, even the UPS deliveryman who checked the jar every day after he'd handed over our packages.

Many of our customers feel a sense of ownership. One customer, Nancy Felker, volunteers to "fluff up our mulch" in the landscaping by the road. She loves this work, it makes the roadside display look fresh and tended, and passersby see what maintenance can do to liven their gardens. A group of women and men called Annie's Angels formed in the early years. They transplanted seedlings, loaded fertilizers for customers, swept the store, tilled the garden, cut flowers for bouquets. In exchange, they earned credits toward purchases, the equivalent of a 10 percent discount. For three years, twelve people blessed Annie's in this way, and one Angel, Beth Best, ended up working for us.

We strive to make a place where people feel at home, and like Fred's, Annie's is modest and unpretentious. The store is thirty feet by forty feet with a shed roof and a six-foot overhang on the front. Built for a farm stand in the late 1970s, the structure had no central heating, and until I moved in 1991, no plumbing. Our two greenhouses are hoop structures covered with plastic sheeting, common among farms in the Pioneer Valley of western Massachusetts.

We have made the most of this simplicity. Painted in warm, Italian colors—terra cotta oranges, light blues and greens, creamy yellows—our little shop invites rest. Every season we decorate our entrance differently—in winter with greens and wreaths, in spring and summer with flowers and vines, in fall with cornstalks and pumpkins. As you walk through our entrance, you see on your left a small water garden landscaped with local, mossy stone. We change the flower displays around the pond throughout the season to keep color there, and in December and through the long winter, we hang white lights on the trees and shrubs surrounding it.

Once you are inside the store, you enjoy delightful and surprising niches and alcoves where Annie's artistic staff tuck treasures—bronze statues, tabletop fountains, dried flowers, and healthy houseplants in beautiful pots. And scattered around the property, in the store and in the greenhouses, are wooden and concrete benches and chairs for you to sit on to view gardens with perennials, ornamental grasses, giant reeds and vegetables, or plants in indoor water ponds.

Annie's has become fuller over the years, a fact not missed by Ann Dorr, an accountant and regular customer. "Like gardens everywhere, Annie's is a work in progress," she said. "On opening day, all the features weren't up and in place. You landscaped the front one year, added the water-garden the next. That's what we do in our backyards. We cut another path; we wait a year until we can afford a piece of garden sculpture; we move things around. A garden evolves. Customers can relate to and be inspired by Annie's evolution."

We pay attention to details and we show this by the creativity and beauty of our displays. We highlight the uniqueness of a product with lighting, placement, and with groupings. We mix textures and colors, heights and shapes. We also have an unusual mix of products from all over the world. Garden stores are often filled with functional items, tools for work. Annie's is filled with items that are functional, but because of the way we display them, we imply that there is more to them than work. There is beauty, there is spirit, there is love of growing plants and being in nature. Julie Gross said, "It's hard to say what is so special about Annie's. It's always just so delightful, somehow, in a down-to-earth sort of way. I suppose there are plenty of people like me who delight in beauty but aren't so good at creating it for themselves. Annie's is ineffable, meaning inexpressible—too sacred to be spoken."

Our customers sense our love of the natural world, and some of them come to Annie's as though to a wellspring. They sniff the dried lavender, they listen to the sounds of water dripping into a pond, they touch ash handles and forged steel tines on tools. They walk underneath arbors, around stone Celtic crosses and into greenhouses. When they leave us, they feel restored. Paola Di Stefano said, "I abandoned traditional religion at a young age, and I have found in the natural world the cycles of birth and death and rebirth that help me to understand myself, my community and the world around me. A visit to Annie's is like seeing these cycles through a magnifying glass. Sometimes I stop by just to feel refreshed, purified, and peaceful."

Annie's replicates, then, some of the characteristics of Fred's and my hometown. We are unpretentious and warm, playful and upbeat. We know our customers and care about them. Still, what is Annie's secret chili recipe? What lures customers to Annie's when competitors like Agway and Wal-Mart are within five minutes' drive? Established independent garden centers are equally close, and specialty growers are ten minutes away. Just as you might ask, What's special about a Fred's hot dog, you might also ask, What's special about Annie's?

Ray Oldenburg, in his book *The Great Good Place*, describes characteristics of places like Fred's and Annie's. They are on neutral ground, welcome all people, are accessible, modest, and playful. Customers develop a sense of ownership for the places, feel restored, at ease and rooted there, and regulars talk freely about their lives, their community, and the world. Great good places unite the community, serve the elderly, bring adults and children together in a relaxed setting, foster democracy, provide places for people to have fun. All of these qualities enhance and encourage friendship, understanding and tolerance.

Even though Annie's demonstrates many of these characteristics, I knew we had to do more than know people, or to make them laugh when they drove by our store. I started asking myself, "What is it most of us need? What are we all longing for?" I did a mental survey of the people I know. Most are working hard and have too little time to relax. Most have enough money and are comfortable physically. But many are taking antidepressants or herbal stress remedies. Most complain that they don't have enough time to be with themselves, or with the people who mean the most to them. As I thought about these people in these situations, I wondered how Annie's might reduce the strains in their lives.

To be in the gardening business is to be lucky, because, as Paola Di Stefano said, gardening connects you to the natural world. It brings you in touch with cycles and weather and problems you can't solve quickly or easily. When you plant a tree, you can't make it grow faster than it wants to grow. You have to be patient, wait and watch. It may take two or three seasons to amend acidic soil in a garden that's been neglected for a number of years. Gardening shows you the processes of nature that are slow and powerful. Ann Dorr said, "Gardening is a nurturing business. I don't think it is an accident that I drifted back to gardening after my special needs child went back to school. I was smart enough to know I needed to stay busy, (and gardening takes up all available time!), but gardening also fills up, to some degree, that nurturing void."

Annie's is a business devoted to organic gardening. We have always promoted sustainable practices, low chemical use, and careful monitoring of plants and their health. How could we combine the spiritual aspects of gardening naturally with the spiritual longing in our customers? How could we develop our business into a place where our customers could rediscover themselves?

Feeding people is one way to do this, and food is often served in great good places. You sit down, you stay awhile, and before you know it, you're talking with one of the regulars about the recent election or complaining about your job. Eating together brings people together. I had seen it happen at Fred's. I always wanted it to happen at Annie's. I was already producing Annie's Own line of jams and jellies, pickles and chutneys, and selling them from the store. From there I had no trouble envisioning people sitting at small café tables drinking tea and eating biscuits served with my orange marmalade. I could hear the chatter and the laughter that would come from such a scene, and I knew it would succeed.

In 1993, we opened a tearoom at Annie's. We didn't have a kitchen, but we got a restaurant permit from the town, bought eight café tables and twenty chairs, and hung a sign. Our vision was to serve herbal teas made from organic herbs we grew in our garden. This would promote gardening, organic methods, and sustenance—all high values at Annie's. We bought scones and biscuits from a local bakery, opened the marmalade, made coffee and tea each morning, and for the next eighteen months, our customers had a place to eat.

The tearoom never generated enough business to keep going, though the people who used it appreciated having a place to meet friends. Sales of our hard goods and plants were growing and we needed the retail space in our 1,200 square foot store. We slowly reduced the number of chairs and tables until none were left, took down the sign, put away the cups and saucers. The next question was, How can we feed people without giving them something to eat?

There is real food, and there is spiritual food. At Annie's, we dole out the latter by giving away a poem with each sale. The idea came from my habit of sharing what I love, and I love poetry because it makes me slow down. I can't hurry and read a poem. If I do, I won't understand it, then I feel frustrated. I also love poetry because I love language, and poetry is word play at its peak.

Since many poets write about gardening and nature in lyrical, humorous, accessible language, I started telling friends about poems, taking poems to dinner parties and reading them aloud, copying them down and mailing them to friends far away. One day I was telling a customer about a poem and I said, "I'll make you a copy and send it to you." And then I thought about giving poems away to everyone. Also I was looking for something to give the customer outside the exchange of money for merchandise. That exchange wasn't enough for me; it left me feeling empty. I wanted something I could hand over that was extra and free, something that would help the customer slow down and relax.

Our community is poetry-friendly. Amherst was the home of Emily Dickinson; Robert Frost taught at Amherst College. Many poets live and write in our area, and poetry readings are common. When I told my friend and poet Mary Clare Powell about my idea, she gave me some of her poems to hand out. Dara Wier brought poems by Theodore Roethke, who'd been a student of hers at UMass. A few years later, she wrote a poem of her own entitled "Evidence of Annie's All Over Town." Henry Lyman, poet and executor for Robert Francis's estate, brought me poems by Francis. James Tate, Sharon Dunn, Gene Zieger, Margaret Robison, and other local poets delivered poems. Customers suggested their favorites, and Wanda Cook wrote six haiku poems about her garden and brought them in. Since 1994, we have given away thousands of poems.

Beautiful words and fresh images can nurture people like gardening and nature can. Interesting combinations of words can surprise and excite readers as quickly as can a beautiful flower or a delicious tomato. Our customers respond to these poems with enthusiasm, taking the poems home and posting them on refrigerators, passing them to friends, inserting them in gifts, reading them to students and their children. Poems are a simple way for Annie's to enrich our customers' busy and fragmented lives.

Still, a poem is a personal, individual experience. Since we've been in business, we have also sought to engage our customers in experiences they could share with other people. We have especially wanted to encourage children to garden and to be aware of the natural world. From 1992 to 1994, we challenged children and adults to a radish contest. We gave one free packet of radish seed to each family or contestant, and told them to come back in six weeks with their product.

The children and adults were more creative than we expected, and contestants came not only with planted radishes, but also with huge papîer-mâché radishes, radish poems and paintings, T-shirts with radishes stenciled on them, radish raps, radish necklaces, and a radish piñata filled with candy for all the other contestants.

In 1995, we invited children to participate in another event that Susan Lehtinen, a customer from Amherst, introduced to us. Susan brought me an article from the children's magazine *Family Fun* titled, "In Celebration of Mud Season: Let your kids jump, roll, and delight in nature's messiest stuff." The article described castles made with mud, mud pools in plastic swimming pools, a crazy obstacle course, a mud pie bake sale. Susan knew we liked to engage children in gardening and nature projects, and she knew we had land.

Our half-acre field is wet in the spring and we can't plant anything in it until the soil dries in April, so we agreed to sponsor a Mud Festival in late March. Susan and I planned activities—a slalom run using bamboo stakes as markers, a tunnel made of sawhorses, two thirty-six-inch hoops to jump through made from old Christmas-wreath rings. Susan brought her kitchen timer, and we organized relay races, a tug-of-war, mud ball throws, and mud pie constructions. Faith Deering brought insects that live in mud and earthworms for an earthworm race.

Some children didn't like the feel of mud on their feet, but enjoyed making mud pies and racing earthworms. Other children couldn't stay away from the mushy stuff. By the end of the afternoon, most were barefoot and covered with mud. We washed them off with the hose and gave everybody honey candy. Susan was pleased with the outcome and our field benefited from much needed aeration. Martha Thompson often visits Annie's with one of her children. She said, "I've enjoyed Annie's over the years for its relaxing, receptive, and creative atmosphere. My children have always felt welcomed and wanted at Annie's." And Paola Di Stefano, mother of two, said, "My children love to visit almost as much as I do— to sniff and pat, to cradle a piece of bunny statuary, to color a picture, to talk to Moses and feed him doggie treats, to stick a little finger under the trickle of a water fountain, to get lost in the labyrinth. A trip to Annie's is always greeted with the same enthusiasm as a trip to the fair."

In 1998, we stumbled onto the idea of a sunflower labyrinth and it turned out to be a great blessing for us, for children, and for all our adult customers. Labyrinths are ancient patterns laid out on the ground with a path that leads to a center. They are not puzzles like mazes are, with tall walls and dead ends. A labyrinth gives you a path to follow and, if you stay on it, you get to the center. Because you are not going anywhere, it is a meditation on patience and trust. You walk in and you walk out, just like breath itself.

I had read an article about labyrinths in the *New York Times* and thought, "I need that," but I didn't see the connection to Annie's. Then a few weeks later, Michelle Wiggins, our gardener, and Ann Gibson, my partner, and I were talking about what to plant in our half-acre plot. The field is visible to traffic, and I wanted as much color there as possible. I suggested sunflowers; Michelle suggested a sunflower labyrinth. I remembered the story in the paper and knew it was the perfect solution.

Ann and Michelle chose a simple design, a seven-course pattern from the palace of Nestor (thirteenth-century B.C.) in Pylos, Greece. The labyrinth had a diameter of seventy feet with 1,000 feet of path. They planted the seed rows four feet apart so Michelle could till between the rows to keep down weeds. Ann, also an artist, placed one of her sculptures made of willow and maple saplings in the center and surrounded her piece with stones. By early August, the flowers had begun to bloom. We sent a press release to the local papers; they all ran some kind of announcement and one paper featured the labyrinth on the front page with a color photograph of the sunflowers. We started fielding calls from people who'd never heard of us before. The response was astonishing.

Why, in this hectic time, are our customers and their friends walking in and out of a circle? People walk our labyrinths for different reasons—meditation, play, to be with friends, to watch honeybees collect pollen, to see chickadees collect seed, to be with their children. They are all searching, as I am searching, for peace of mind and beauty, for self-knowledge and understanding. I don't know if they or I will find these in our labyrinth, but our labyrinth gives them another place to seek it. And because Annie's provides this kind of place, our customers know how much we care about them and their well-being.

Many retail businesses in our area keep animals on the premises, and our dog Moses was a part of Annie's from the time he was born in 1992 until he died in May 2001. Moses was a forty-pound mongrel with beagle markings who loved children and adults. He greeted customers with enthusiasm, turned over on his back for children to scratch his chest, chased sticks thrown by anyone. Children and adults came to Annie's just to see Moses (many brought dog biscuits), and children often drew his portrait for our children's bulletin board. Occasionally a customer picked him up and took him for a walk in a nearby nature preserve. One couple photographed their two kids, arms around Moses, in front of our winter decorations, and used the photo for their Christmas card. Ann Dorr said, "Moses was a very important part of Annie's. Strangers came in, saw Moses, and immediately relaxed. This is a far cry from shopping at a sterile superstore." When he died, we announced it on our sign and dozens of customers sent condolences.

At Annie's, education is our most precious commodity. I am a teacher. I like to watch people learn and I enjoy encouraging people to solve problems. Gardeners are perpetual learners, and there is so much to know about plants, soil science, pest control, design, harvesting, and crafting. Cooperative extension services have been cut, and new gardeners don't live near relatives who can teach them the basics. Since 1991, we had addressed ourselves to this need by producing a newsletter about gardening and crafting, and by leading over thirty workshops a year. Our workshops focus on specific plant types (bamboo, roses, bulbs, perennials, etc.), gardening techniques (organics, container and water gardening, for example), spirituality (aromatherapy, fountain design, garden writing, herbal medicines), and crafting (wreath making, herbal salves, etc.).

Many speakers have led workshops at Annie's on heirloom plants, unusual daffodils, edible flowers, landscaping with stone, making rustic trellises. In the middle of winter, we've invited poets to read their poetry about gardening and nature, and during spring singer/songwriters have serenaded our customers. Local English Morris Dance troupes bless Annie's each spring and fall with bells and songs of praise. We have sponsored field trips to the New England Flower Show in Boston and to private gardens in Vermont and western Massachusetts. We tap the resources around us, look for competencies all around our region, and bring that intelligence to Annie's.

Learning to succeed at something—whether it is flower arranging or seed starting—gives confidence. This confidence spills into other parts of our lives. If I can design a perennial border, I can approach that client whose account

I want. If I can make my own Christmas wreath, I bet I can make other things with my hands. Ann Dorr said, "I have learned so much at Annie's through the workshops. I count on them to give me new ideas, remind me of a few basics, and generally inspire me for the season to come."

As our customers become more competent, they become better customers. They appreciate handmade items and understand how much skill is involved in making them. They embrace the value of a well-grown, pest-free plant and look forward to continuing its care in their own organic garden. They know how to manage diseases and don't ask us to supply harmful pesticides and herbicides. Informed, intelligent, and confident customers make us a better business.

Better businesses reach out. Our community includes people who are not well off or comfortable, and Annie's responds to them in a variety of ways. To benefit a local women's shelter one year, we sponsored a Gingerbread Woman Contest at Christmas. We have supported our local food bank and survival center by contributing a percentage of our sales for a day or a week, selling their cookbooks and Christmas cards. We donate goods to parent/teacher associations, libraries, and scout troops. We underwrite public radio, a college chorus, the university's fine arts program, and local theater groups. Ann Dorr says, "When you held the Amherst Survival Center benefit, I came in and picked up their brochure to find out what their hours were. I had been meaning to get some clothes over there for months, and Annie's inspired me to get it done. That commitment to community impressed me, and made me more committed."

At Annie's, we try to be a good neighbor. We listen to the cries of the spirit, the hungers of the body, the longings of all ages to be seen, to be known, to be loved and challenged. We respond in ways a retail business can—with beauty, with attention to detail, with honest education, with interesting products at good prices, with patience, with creativity, and with humor. Keith Hollingworth has thought about this aspect of Annie's and said, "I am an artist, a painter. One question I ask my students is, 'What is beauty?' They struggle with a definition and each one is specifically unique, but a consensus emerges of a feeling inside, a good, wholesome, intangible, transcendent feeling. It is a feeling of the moment, of here, now, and of place. Annie's is a place of the special moment."

Annie's has evolved from the work of a group of people. It is not the creation of one or two people Our staff has made Annie's responsive, funny, creative, and alive. Everybody who works at Annie's plays with the sign. Everybody learns about plants. Everybody contributes to problem solving. My favorite question is "What do you think?" and we ask that of everyone who works at Annie's. We have been lucky. The right people at the right time have come to work on this project, and our success is due to their commitment and vision. They make Annie's magic; they are Annie's secret ingredient.

Will people hunger for businesses that address these needs in the new millennium? Will any of this matter? I don't know, but I believe so. We human beings haven't changed all that much since I was growing up in Smithfield. Places like Fred's and Creech's, and now Annie's and all the other examples in this book, will always be places we remember as special and formative. In them, people know our names, and use them. In them, we have a place and we know it. Through them, we find our way in our society. Third place or third base—both are close to home.

Rugs are imported, displayed, and sold out of the Third Place Coffeehouse by local weavers.

The Third Place Coffeehouse

RALEIGH, NORTH CAROLINA

IN 1996, Richard Futrell wrote me explaining how he'd come to open The Third Place coffeehouse in Raleigh, North Carolina. He was a man in quest of an answer. Unlike some authors presented here who hale from habitats of hospitality in the Old South, Richard spent his college years in a northern city where he found people anything but hospitable. His reading amounted to "a desperate search to figure out why people act the way they do at a time when there are more people around them than ever before, they have plenty to eat, plenty to do, they are relatively safe and well taken care of. Basically, I was trying to figure out why people have become so unhappy and downright nasty."

While employed as a retail sales manager, Richard adopted a policy of "killing 'em with kindness," and was determined to win over anyone who would "come in off the street bound and determined to spread their misery in my shop." On one memorable occasion, a "mean and nasty" older woman was won over and left with a smile only to return a few minutes later with an ice cream cone in each hand, "one for me as an apology for her behavior and a token of appreciation for mine."

Richard needed a place where he could work his magic, not only to the betterment of a few individuals here and there, but to the betterment of the human community. He realized it wouldn't be easy but worthwhile endeavors rarely are.

My introduction to *The Great Good Place* occurred in the early 1990s as I scoured the labyrinthine stacks of the Chicago library. I was a young man in search of answers. Standing at the library's huge gothic windows, I looked out on the crowded, bustling city and wondered,

"Why are all those people so lonely?" We, as citizens of one of the largest and most crowded cities in the world, are literally living on top of each other. We bump into each other on the streets, stand in line together at the bank, and sit in each other's laps on the train. With so much daily contact, how could we possibly be so lonely?

This is what I wanted to know. I had studied psychology in college and worked in the field for years, and the most common complaint I heard was "I am lonely." When I talked to my friends who had recently been scattered across the continent during the great post-college diaspora, I heard the same thing —lonely, isolated, bored. It was a general malaise! A national phenomenon! And I, with my youthful enthusiasm and naïveté, was going to find the answer. And I thank you Ray Oldenburg, for leading the way.

REALITY

Seven years and many seventy-hour weeks later, I think I am still pretty thankful to Ray for the inspiration and direction offered in his epic tome of revolutionary social theory, *The Great Good Place*. The truth is I was very lonely at the time myself and, as a student of social theory and frequenter of the myriad coffeehouses in Chicago, *The Great Good Place* simply struck a chord in my bored Gen-X heart. It spoke to me. I was inspired.

So I took to the road with an accomplice and set off to the golden South, the new land of opportunity, North Carolina. Here, with the help of a partner I had only just met (and on the back porch of a rural farmhouse, to boot!), I was going to simultaneously live my version of the great American dream *and* enrich the lives of the residents of Raleigh, North Carolina.

As I look back now on our naïvete and inexperience, I realize that it must have been the sheer force of youthful excitement and enthusiasm of my partner Ty Beddingfield and I that convinced everyone from the bankers to the landlord to our first few customers that we were for real. Hell, *we* were convinced. Our eyes ablaze with passionate zeal, we had not only a plan, but a philosophy! Ray's name was always on our lips, a copy of *The Great Good Place* close at hand, and a stack of photocopied essays I wrote, entitled "What Is a Third Place?," ready to stuff into the hands or pastry sacks of the mildly interested.

Somehow it all worked. Ty is fond of telling people who commented on the high failure rate of restaurants; "Oh, we failed all right, we just kept showing up to work!"

And this is true. Over the past five years, we have learned quite a bit about business, taxes, real estate, budgeting, forecasting, cost analysis, tax planning, insurance, management, and old junky pickup trucks. It was trial by fire but we kept showing up, guided more by the principles of *The Great Good Place* than by sound business practice. We could have thrown in the towel on many occasions, but we really had no idea, so we just kept showing up. Luckily, it has all worked out and we still have a job. And we have learned volumes.

I have learned that, yes, there is a general malaise in America and it is worse than I had previously thought. I never thought people would recognize the social importance of our coffeehouse. I thought it would be more like a social petri dish with Ty and I spying on the progress of our experiment; the customers, our subjects, acting out the various tenets laid out in our hypothesis/business plan.

The truth is, people noticed immediately the benefits of having such a place in their neighborhood. I am still shocked at how often people approach me simply to say "Thank you," not for having good coffee or sandwiches but simply for opening the place. It has become important to them, their neighborhood, and their sense of place.

This "sense of place" and the intangibles that make such a place are difficult to quantify. The actual process of making good food and drinks is important, but in reality, it's the easiest part. The atmosphere, both physical and social, is the trickiest and most essential part of creating a warm and welcoming third place. Both need constant attention and periodic tweaking. Both show signs of neglect and fatigue immediately.

Through our experience we have learned that it all begins with us, Ty and me, and our attitudes concerning ourselves, our coworkers, and our customers. We have discovered that our attitudes are transparent and have a very powerful effect on the feel and impression of the business and physical space. As the figureheads and persons in charge, we set the emotional tone and interactive parameters. Simply acting in a respectful and positive manner, it is possible to transmit to our co-workers acceptable modes of conduct that are in line with our philosophy. There is no need for preaching or listing acceptable behaviors or beating down personality with a handbook of acceptable greeting, dress codes, and behaviors.

We have always hired people with strong personalities. In fact, the only true criterion necessary to work at the Third Place is that one is a nice person—period.

The rest can be learned in a day or two. We have consistently relied upon the interesting and colorful personalities of our co-workers at the Third Place to keep the atmosphere intriguing, fresh and new. All of the people who have worked with us over the years have taught me something about my business, myself, and the world around me at some point during their tenure, contributing problem-solving skills and for this I am grateful.

Every employee is a potential wellspring of new ideas, or perhaps simply a needed boost of positive attitude to the dynamic mix of personalities. We have up to twenty employees at a time at the Third Place, ranging in age from sixteen to forty. This has proved to be a very rich mix of interests, backgrounds, attitudes, personal styles, beliefs, tastes, and tolerances. These people have proven to be what the Third Place is truly about—bringing together all sorts of people under one roof to work and live and play and just be together under no pretense or set guidelines whatsoever. The outcome is truly magical and I feel incredibly honored to have been a part of it. As the owner and creator, I am not central to this creation but peripheral, as it has become a beast of its own, one that I can simply oversee, nourish, and tend to.

Just as Ty and I set the mode and tone of the place through example for our employees, they, in turn do the same through contact over the counter with the customers. I have always marveled at the connection created between individuals through short, good-natured, daily, informal contact. As Ray points out in his book, this is the essential aspect of a third place that has disappeared from the American social landscape.

This natural social chain of events continues as the customers pick up from the employees, rather subversively I might add, a certain casual socialness that manifests itself in a greeting, nod, wink, or even light conversation with the people around them. Whereas we are used to keeping our social blinders on in modern retail situations, the atmosphere of a third place, both physical and social, fosters a convivial openness. This openness, however, should not be confused with a contact or therapy group, since people are not required to be social, only invited to be so.

As Ray states in *The Great Good Place*, the nature of a third place is one in which the presence of a "regular" is always welcome, although never required. Membership is a simple, fluid process of frequent social contact, renewed each time by choice of the people involved. Eventually, social bonds develop through a type of informal intimacy. The important aspect of these relationships is that they occur outside of any commitment and exist solely in the realm of basic human respect. I ascribe huge importance to this one point because it is this one valuable kernel that is slipping away from our isolated modern world. I think that we all miss its presence and this affects us all in very slight, painful ways.

Basic human respect is communicated best not through any law or religious text, but through daily, informal social contact with the people around us. Basic human respect is passed on to succeeding generations most effectively not through law enforcement and punishment but through modeling, such that your children may act as you do, think as you do, do as you do. A bit frightening, isn't it?

So the next time you're picking up your mail, getting gas, or getting coffee, raise your eyes from your shoes, try a grin, and say "hello" to the person across from you. They just might surprise you.

Local residents enjoy a game of chess at Crossroads.

Crossroads

LAKE FOREST PARK, WASHINGTON

I MET Ron Sher a few years ago when he invited me to the grand open-ing of Third Place Books in Lake Forest Park, a suburb of Seattle. While I was there, he took me over to Bellevue, the community in which his pet project is located. A dozen years ago he became the key figure in trans-forming a failed shopping center into a highly successful community center. Here he tells how it was done. I have subsequently revisited Crossroads and I still have trouble believing what I see. It is filled with people of all ages and nationalities in an atmosphere resembling carnival time. I refer to Ron as "the miracle worker from Medina," for this is not his only triumph.

When we visit one of his projects, he parks as far from the entrance as possible so as not to deprive a customer of easier parking, and when we walk through the place, he stoops to pick up litter. You'd never know this gentle, soft-spoken, friendly man is the "big cheese."

The Crossroads story is one that involves many people, and many changes. In a traditional case study it would be about the redevel-opment of a 380,000 square foot retail shopping center with a 170,000 square foot interior mall. The mall was struggling with a high crime rate, which caused many of the tenants to leave and the remaining ones to per-form poorly, and extensive repairs and maintenance were necessary. This is the story of the transformation of this property into a successful 460,000 square foot center, that is now the vibrant heart of a communi-ty. The revitalization of the Crossroads has made a huge difference in the spirit of the community by allowing a sense of pride to flourish, creating a strong housing demand, and restoring its image as a desirable place to live. It is also the story of coming of age of a third place. Literally thousands of people use Crossroads as a third place, and it's unique in that there are several third places that are all part of this greater one.

SETTING THE SCENE

The Crossroads neighborhood is the easternmost part of Bellevue, Washington, a wealthy suburb east of Seattle on the other side of Lake Washington. Crossroads is the most ethnically and economically diverse area in Bellevue. Until the construction of the two bridges across Lake Washington it was a sleepy suburban neighborhood. Since then Bellevue has grown rapidly and now has an office and technology center nearly equal to that of Seattle. In the Crossroads neighborhood the main area zoned for the commercial center consisted of approximately sixty acres, of which the Crossroads Shopping Center represented forty acres at the intersection of 8th and 156th Avenue N.E. Today this is a major intersection with over forty thousand cars passing through each day. Most of the property was bought by home builders, including the commercial site. From the late 1950s through the late 1960s developers built tract homes in the area and multifamily homes near the commercial site. The development of the commercial center, which eventually became the Crossroads Shopping Center and in fact gave the neighborhood its name, stemmed from the desire to fulfill the retail needs of this new community. The center grew as the demand for goods and services grew, and more and more shops were built without a cohesive plan. An effort was made to upgrade the center in the early 1980s by enclosing a portion of the buildings to create an interior mall, but this proved to be unsuccessful in attracting new tenants and business, and the center was placed on the market.

Crossroads was bought by a group of syndicators who believed the center could be reinvigorated by transforming part of the interior mall into a public market similar to Pike Street in Seattle, or Granville Island in Canada, which they spent the next two years trying to accomplish. The group underestimated the difficulty of leasing the center, of creating the critical mass necessary for success, the type of intense management necessary to implement the Public Market concept, and the effort required to overcome the center's strong negative image. Finally the partnership had to be restructured, and my brother Merritt and I took over as managing partners. I accepted the day-to-day responsibilities, since I lived fifteen minutes from the project, but Merritt and I consulted on major issues.

After taking over the development of Crossroads we had to figure out how to make it successful. It was clear that we could never compete with Bellevue Square, which is one of the premier centers in the country and only four miles away. To make things worse, Bellevue Square had a competition clause in their leases that prevented any of their tenants from leasing within five miles. We were also one and a half miles away from the 520 freeway and three miles from 405, and the national chain retailers preferred freeway access and visibility. Until we had more credibility and critical mass to attract customers, leasing would be tough. We needed to figure out what we had going for us and how we could compete. As we saw it, the center had several assets: we were located in the downtown of the Crossroads area and had thirty thousand people in our primary trade area; we had forty acres of property that, if used properly, could really have a positive impact on the surrounding neighborhoods; we had strong community support, and we had what some people considered a liability—density and ethnic and economic diversity.

Looking at this we decided that first and foremost we needed to become the downtown of East Bellevue. We needed to satisfy all the needs of the neighborhood. We also decided that all the urban energy that many considered detrimental to our success should be welcomed and celebrated. The Public Market, though it had not been financially successful, had begun to attract the attention of our neighbors. We decided to try and make it the catalyst for the gathering of people that occurs in a downtown. It was apparent to everyone living in the area that the development at Crossroads had stalled. Therefore we felt it was important to change the public's perception of the center. The first thing we needed to do after assuming control was to make a positive statement to show people that things were starting to happen. To this end, we demolished three buildings at the main corner of the project on 8th Street and 156th

Avenue N.E. This marked the beginning of our orchestration to create momentum and change public opinion.

Another early step was to go to the mayor and introduce ourselves. We invited all key department heads and city council members to visit Crossroads and talked to them about our planned changes. By the end of the meeting they were surprised that we had no specific requests. We did, however, have some issues that were vitally important and we needed to make them clear. We needed to convey that we had a problem, and that it was in both of our interests to make Crossroads successful. We needed to act as a team. As developers, Merritt and I wanted no special favors. What we did want was to develop a spirit of cooperation and teamwork and a "can-do" attitude.

An example of the type of partnership we eventually formed can be seen in the compromise we reached regarding the major Crossroads sign. We wanted to place a "Crossroads" sign on the main corner and at the same time create a small garden and public space around it. At first consideration the city told us that this was not allowed under city code. But with some creative brainstorming and mutual cooperation, the city eventually determined that they could approve it as a "community identification" sign.

HOW WE MADE IT HAPPEN

Crossroads has been a major redevelopment project, and the enormous amount of detail involved is enough to put even me to sleep. However, some of these details are particularly relevant in their impact on the development and success of the Public Market and the redevelopment of the center as a whole.

For instance, once we had demolished the corner buildings, we decided to design a special 16,000 square foot building that would set the tone for the center. We went far beyond the requirements of our tenant, Blockbuster Video, and took special care not to back the new building to either the street or the center, thus creating storefronts on both sides. Another important development in the project was the completion of a new 42,000 square foot eight screen multiplex cinema that was for a period the number one cinema in the state. This, of course, did much to attract people to Crossroads and the Public Market. Next we demolished the old four-screen cinema and constructed a new wing to the mall adjacent to the Public Market. This allowed an expansion of the Public Market, a large skylight with seating under it, and a 38,000 square foot upscale supermarket as well as several other stores, all connecting to the Public Market.

We also felt it was very important to have tenant activity, even to the extent that if we could not attract a tenant, we would create one. In order to attract tenants, we needed to remodel the exterior. It was dated and monolithic, and it sent the wrong message to the public. It made Crossroads look dull, old, vacant, and unsafe. But we could not find a tenant for the most prominent corner of the enclosed mall. Finally we discovered someone who had been in the children's clothing business and wanted to open another store, but didn't have the resources. We formed a partnership, which our development group funded, and planned an exciting 6,500 square foot store for him. After he failed, we took it over and operated it until selling it to the current manager. She is still at Crossroads today and has opened another successful store in a different shopping center. We opened a music store until we could attract Blockbuster Music, a toy store until we could find the right tenant for that space, and today we still operate a daycare with play equipment, which allows customers to do their shopping unencumbered by their children. All of these retail ventures were essential to maintain the forward motion of the redevelopment of Crossroads and to support our existing tenants.

BUILD IT, AND THEY WILL COME

Vitality is an essential element in attracting customers to a shopping center, and it's also a very important characteristic of a third place. Clearly, the most important ingredient of vitality is the presence of people. Our dilemma was how to attract customers. One of my staff had seen a large chess set in Vancouver, British Columbia, and suggested that we have one made for the market. We found a wood craftsman who constructed a beautiful wooden chess set. The pawns are fourteen inches high and the King and Queen thirty inches and twenty-eight inches, respectively. The game is played on an eight-foot chessboard. We promoted the set with tournaments and had famous chess masters come to play in tournaments. Even world chess champion Anatoly Karpov made an appearance. The chess set became an important part of the entire Crossroads image and Crossroads as a center of the local chess community. There are always several games in progress and at times as many as twenty. The chess set is very symbolic in that it shows the community that they can feel comfortable in coming to Crossroads just to hang out, and they don't have to spend money to be welcome.

Over time the Public Market at Crossroads has changed from stands offering a variety of produce, vegetables, fish, and meats to restaurants and eateries. One aspect that I feel has helped the Crossroads Public Market to work so well as a third place is the size of the common area. Over time seating has grown to accommodate almost one thousand people. The area includes two large connected seating areas with many smaller ones tucked in among the restaurants. These seating configurations allow people to be private, to be in the middle of things, or on the periphery. Through the chess set, free entertainment, a magazine stand, and a variety of community events, we make a conscious effort to send out the message to our customers that they are welcome.

At the entrance to the Public Market was a 5,500 square foot space that had at one point been a restaurant, then later an unsuccessful part of the Public Market. We were approached by a used bookstore called Half-Price Books about the possibility of leasing this space. They were a chain based in Dallas, Texas, and at that time operated a small store in downtown Bellevue. Their presentation was quite "bare bones," and although we questioned the efficacy of putting this tenant at our front door, we decided to take a chance. We felt that the ability to browse coupled well with hanging out, and that one would complement the other. Now their chain has over sixty stores and I believe that the Crossroads location may be their highest sales per square foot. This has gone a long way toward reinforcing the "come visit us" image we try to project.

While in France on business, my brother Merritt, our French investor, Bertrand Hermite, and I found a nineteenth-century replica of an early-eighteenth-century fountain at a Paris flea market. We bought it and had it shipped to Crossroads. We redesigned the area at the entrance with wrought iron fences, outdoor furniture, a large mural of a park scene behind the fountain and beautiful new landscaping. This provided not only a welcoming space to hang out in, but also a statement about the transformation of Crossroads. It sent a clear message to the merchants that we were not a second-class center. It showed the customers that this was a special place for them, not just an ordinary shopping center. It may seem apparent, but at this stage in the redevelopment we were still working on our identity. Here was another improvement we could promote, and we got some good press coverage from it. It was another small step toward attracting new tenants.

One of the smallest but most important tenants at Crossroads is our Mini City Hall. It is staffed with knowledgeable, energetic Bellevue City employees and with an assisting staff of volunteers. They make a strong effort not only to serve everyone, but also to offer all types of services, especially to our immigrant population. Together with the local community college and Crossroads management they created a program to teach English as a second language, which is conducted right at the Center in its community room. The community room is also made available to tenants, the public, and local nonprofit organizations.

About seven years ago we invited the police to open a substation on the property. We are really happy with that decision, not because the Crossroads environment at this point required the immediate presence of a police force, but because it helped allay any lingering fears and doubts that may have been left over from the problems of the past. It was so satisfying to see how large a number of policemen applied for the three spots available in the substation.

Another major attraction of the Public Market is the free entertainment. Though it started small, the music program has developed a life of its own. At this point we have free entertainment three to four nights a week. We offer everything from acoustic music at "Café Crossroads" to an open-mike night. This is an expensive program for the Center to maintain, but it has been well received. We have a sophisticated sound system, and in addition to having a great reputation with the audiences, we are also known as a great venue for the musicians. Throughout the year we hold many neighborhood festivals and events ranging from a Cultural Crossroads Fair, which is a celebration of the neighborhood's ethnic and cultural diversity, to Rose festivals and ugly dog shows.

When trying to visualize and understand the elements necessary to create the kind of energy and interaction that I wanted at the Crossroads Public Market, one guiding principle I have used is Ray Oldenburg's concept of the third place, which I discovered in 1993 in his book *The Great Good Place*. After reading his book, I realized that we had been trying to create a third place all along, even though we had never even heard of one. Ray's book helped us fine-tune what we were doing. It helped us articulate what we wanted Crossroads to be and allowed us to explain to the neighborhood how our goals for the Crossroads could help to enrich the community.

I believe we have done many of the kinds of things that Ray champions, and if he visited Crossroads today, he would indeed find a great good place. We continue to remain consistent and driven in our efforts to make Crossroads the downtown center for the surrounding community. We want it to be a place where people can come to eat, drink, shop, play, read, or just hang out for a few hours and feel completely comfortable and welcome. I believe that Crossroads works as a third place on so many different levels, and with the continuing support and encouragement from the community, it will only get better.

Debby Culp and Russell McCracken (center) visit while Henry Klush and his dog Marcus relax. Henry and Marcus are regular fixtures in front of Horizon Books in the warmer months.

Horizon Books

TRAVERSE CITY, MICHIGAN

DRUGSTORES, BOOKSTORES, coffee shops, and other independent retail operations that once served widely as local gathering places are being replaced by mammoth, impersonal chain operations. Though opposition to these community-destroying behemoths is mounting, they continue to grow and independent operators continue to fall under their onslaught.

In this context, it has been gratifying to learn that an association of independent bookstore owners has found the third place theme useful in defending themselves against the giants. "Vic" Herman's Horizon Books is a third place in the best tradition of local bookstores, and though Traverse City is not exactly a metropolis, he is widely recognized for his acumen in the world of books and for his devotion to the community.

To write about Horizon Books, Mr. Herman called upon an old friend and professional scribe, Paul LaPorte. After Paul completed his task, he called to tell me what joy he experienced in writing about the store, its owner, and the family. When I spoke with him he had recently taken a trip to points south and found himself one evening in a rollicking Cajun third place in Lafayette, Louisiana. He loved it!

"You cannot create a place like this, it just sort of happens." This is how Vic Herman describes Horizon Books, in Traverse City, Michigan, when he is asked about the third place aspects of his bookstore. He makes it seem as though this downtown Front Street venue has somehow evolved accidentally into the popular cross-generational gathering place it has become. To visit and get to know the store is to discover that this may not be entirely true. In fact, the bright and intensely private Vic Herman is the primary force behind this wonderful public gathering place.

Horizon Books has been a downtown focal point and anchor store in Traverse City for nearly forty years. Now, it has two satellite stores in the nearby communities of Cadillac and Petoskey. (The company was featured in the March/April 1999 issue of Independent Publisher in an article titled: "Horizon Books, Striving to be 'The Third Place.'") Even though the company has grown and succeeded in the face of changing demographics and retail competition from the large chains, it has continued its success and retained a family feeling of a retailer uniquely dedicated to serving the community. "Our store has always been devoted to this idea of community," explains Herman.

Horizon Books is much more than a bookstore. When you walk through the door, you are likely to see one of the groups that use the facility. Reading discussion groups, writing groups, children's story hour groups, Toastmasters, and others regularly meet in the hundred-seat Horizon Shine Café at no charge. You may hear poetry, music, or a speaker as you walk through the aisles of well-chosen titles; or see friends using the store as a meeting spot. One unique recent event was a bridal shower, where the friends of the book-loving bride-to-be used the store as both a shopping venue and a unique location for her celebration.

Since Traverse City is a tourist destination on the shores of Lake Michigan, visitors from outside the area regularly visit the store. Many of the visitors have expressed the feeling of "humanness" they experience. They fondly describe the staff and customer-to-customer contact and interaction they have when they visit the store. One visitor told us that a visit to Traverse City would not be complete without a stop at Horizon Books. "The entire experience is quite friendly and unlike anything else we find in the city."

BACK WHERE IT ALL BEGAN

How did this all happen? It began on a farm in Suttons Bay, fifteen miles north of Traverse City, where Vic Herman grew up. He had an adventurous Huck Finn childhood and, as one of six children, he shared a bike with his older brother until his grandpa gave him a '31 Chevy. His childhood memories are of a community that worked together for a common good. Everyone worked on chores, and Vic smiles when he remembers times spent hunting, trapping, butchering, and helping preserve wild fruit. When he was six, he remembers watching his family home burn to the ground as neighbors and volunteers worked together, risking their own safety to help save a neighbor.

Vic was a kid who was able and allowed to express himself in those gathering places he fondly recalls. Since there was no local or rural delivery, the local post office was a place where people met to discuss the comings and goings of the day. This forum was not age or gender specific and one might run into just about anyone there and discuss just about anything. The two gathering places that stand out most for Vic, however, are the barbershop and his grandpa's auto repair shop. Each favored a free cross-generational exchange of ideas.

"It's not that I went to the barbershop to hang around, but, as a teenager, whenever I went to get a haircut, there was an ongoing conversation I could participate in. It could have been about sports or hunting, or about local issues. It was not a gossipy place." Vic explains, "It didn't matter that I was a kid—I could express myself and I enjoyed that." In the winter, the local cherry farmers, without much to do, would fill the dozen or so chairs that lined the walls and spend time discussing the issues and simply being together in a welcome, friendly environment. Often, there was no intention of a haircut, but—young or old—everyone was included in the conversation in a meaningful way. "There were always three or four men there and often as many as eight or ten," Vic explains. "I felt safe and at home in this expressive, male, adult environment. I learned a lot and was able to add something once in a while."

Grandpa's auto repair shop was about halfway to town from the Herman farm and provided a convenient stopping-off place for young Vic. "Grandfather was great with kids." Vic recalls, fondly. "The place was more than an auto repair shop. It was also a gathering place where the regulars always had a euchre game going on in the back room. In the fall, we helped make cider and wine on Grandfather's memorable old press.

An eight by ten foot side room was transformed into sort of a grocery. It was a predecessor to today's convenience markets, only this one had car seats to sit on and a Coke machine that operated on the honor system. Sure, Grandfather was in the auto repair business, but that's not the only reason most of the people were there."

The seeds for Horizon Books were planted in 1961, when Vic was a Michigan State University graduate student in East Lansing, funded by the GI Bill after an undergraduate ROTC program and three years in the Air Force. Vic was feeding his voracious appetite for learning with a potpourri of classes in math, languages, physics, philosophy, and economics. His curiosity had been ignited and if he spotted a course that interested him, he signed up for it. Sometimes, he would audit the classes without credit, just to feed this curiosity. Married and with a young family, he supplemented his GI Bill income with entrepreneurial college town projects.

He and his wife, Nancy, and a friend got the notion to start a bookstore in Traverse City, and they bought six hundred square feet of retail space on Front Street. His friend went north to run the store and Vic did all the ordering from East Lansing. "I was having the time of my life," Vic said, "I could take any class I wanted and I enjoyed buying the books that interested me. I got pure joy out of going through the catalogs and buying books. For the first time in my life, I could satiate my intellectual curiosity." Apparently, this knack for buying books has served Vic well, since nearly everyone comments on the unique selection of titles at Horizon Books. The early years were tough, but from the beginning, Vic realized that his business was more than books. His orientation was broader than mere product. Great selection, long hours, and attention to the customer led to a steady and recurring clientele. "Our store has been devoted to this idea of community," he says, "We've always wanted to be a gathering place where people stop in and meet other people."

A FAMILY AFFAIR

Horizon Books has been a family affair from the beginning. Vic's kids grew up in the store, coming in when they wanted. The eldest, Pam, was involved with the store almost from the beginning. Both she and her younger sister, Susan, managed the Petoskey outlet at different times. Vic's two youngest, Eric and Erica, often would run the cash register alone as teenagers. Erica enjoyed the Sunday morning shift and opened and ran the store by herself, developing her own rapport with that segment of their clientele. This was at a time when she and Eric had to use a step stool to reach the cash register. It wasn't long before Eric and Erica were in charge of the children's book department. They felt comfortable with recommendations, since they had just read and enjoyed some of these titles only a few years earlier. Amy, Vic's current wife, tells a story about Fiona, the daughter of a recent employee. She was only ten years old when she would come to work with her mother. One day, when a customer was asking about some suitable children's titles, Marti, Fiona's mother, told her: "Fiona can probably help you better than I can." At first, the startled customer was put off by the sales assistance from a ten-year-old. When she left the store an hour or so later with an armload of books, she thanked Amy and told her that Fiona "knew as much about children's books as anyone else in the store."

Today, two of Vic's four children are still in the business. Pamela Herman Anderson is the book buyer and Vic describes her as having the same love of books that he has. Erica Ankerson heads the accounting department. Susan and Eric are in other businesses and have moved away from the area. Sadly, Vic's wife Nancy passed away in 1979.

Sales and marketing manager Amy Reynolds also works with Vic as part of the family. In her first job out of college, armed with a degree in English, she joined Horizon Books and lived with the Hermans in town. From her very first interview with Vic's daughter, Susan, Amy felt like a part of the family. She joined the staff and has never left. Part of the family? Yes—in a very special way. A few years ago, she married her boss, Vic Herman. Together, with other family members and a talented staff, they continue to operate a successful and friendly company in spite of today's retail pressures. Vic makes it a priority to cultivate an excellent rapport with his employees. Of the employees who are not family, it seems that several have been with the Hermans long enough to qualify for family status. Bob Breithaupt is chief receiving clerk and has been with Horizon

Books for twenty-nine years. Lois Orth brings thirty years of bookselling experience to Horizon. The Petoskey store has been under the consistent hand of Maggie Poxson for twenty years. All of these long-timers have a dedication to books and to people who enjoy books.

CUSTOMER LOYALTY

𝒥𝓉'𝓼 clear that the community spirit imparted by Horizon Books has made an impact not only on Vic's family and employees but also on the loyal patrons who have helped elevate the store to the third place haven it has become.

Howard Hintze remembers the early days. He moved to northern Michigan thirty-four years ago, when Horizon Books was the only bookstore in town. That year, he began teaching at Interlochen Academy, a nationally known arts-related private school a few miles from Traverse City. Fresh from a stint in the Peace Corps in Borneo, and with little money, he relied on Vic as a guide and Horizon Books as a resource for his course work, teaching eleventh and twelfth grade English literature. He remembers the Herman kids working in the store, reminding him of his father's grocery in Iowa in the 1940s. "It was a friendly gathering place and they made you feel like family," he recalls. "Often, when I had little or no money, I would sit right on the floor and read as clerks and customers alike stepped over me without saying a thing." He also notes that trustworthiness was always a factor at the store. "When Vic knew I had no money, he would 'put it on the spindle' for me," referring to the old-fashioned retail spindle on the counter for credit slips. It was just the way his father treated customers in his own childhood.

Hintze also felt that Horizon Books was the bridge between Traverse City and the rest of the world because at the time, it was the only place in town where one could buy a *New York Times* or other periodicals not found in rural northern Michigan. He told us: "Vic and Nancy and the kids always took a personal interest in me and my travels and what I was teaching, no matter how busy the store was." He has always been impressed by the unique selection of titles in the store and states his fierce loyalty to Horizon Books by explaining that any visit to Traverse City would not be complete without a stop at Horizon—even if he doesn't need any books.

Tom Shea is a mediator who teaches mediation and conflict management. He has always been interested in progressive issues and is also a regular at Horizon Books. He started coming into Horizon Books in the 1960s when progressive thinking was often divisive. His impression of Vic and the store echoes that of many others who praise the selection of titles. "Vic has always had the uncanny ability to select the right books: the books I like." he explains. "Often, in the '60s and '70s, there were titles that were not 'safe' and other booksellers would not carry them. Horizon Books has always been a venue for free expression of ideas and even public speaking. Vic has been defending free expression as long as I have known him." That is exactly as Vic wants it. "We cannot involve our values in the bookstore," says Vic, "We don't entertain any form of censorship."

Shea also enjoys Horizon's long hours of operation. "You can always count on them being open, even in a snowstorm." There is a particular snowstorm that reminds Tom of an amusing story. It was the biggest storm of the year: January 1977. Everyone in town awoke to covered houses, clogged roads and a thick, deep snow that stopped everything. Everything, that is, except Horizon Books. When Shea strapped on his skis and headed out for his morning visit to Horizon Books, he was not at all surprised (although secretly mildly amused) that the store was open for business as usual. The next day, there was a story in the *Detroit Free Press* by the northern Michigan correspondent, Tom BeVier, about the incident: one single customer skied into Horizon Books to find business as usual. It was like the heartbeat of a small town.

Adair Correll is a local musician who also runs a property management company. He spearheads a group of songwriters who have been meeting in the Horizon Shine Café for over three years called the Northern Michigan Songwriters in the Round. The group has grown to more than thirty members. Originally, there were a few who met to compare their music and jam with one another. As the informal experiences became more regular, they began attracting a consistent crowd and the jam sessions took on the look and feel of performances. The liner notes on the group's recent CD, entitled *New Horizons*, include: "We [Vic and Amy] created Horizon Shine Café in response to customer requests for a community performance space where lectures, demonstrations, meetings, poetry, music, and other cultural events take place regularly. . . . Horizon Shine Café is also the home of Northern Michigan Songwriters in the Round. Their variety, talent, and obvious enjoyment help make Horizon Shine Café the fun gathering place that it is today. Horizon Books is pleased to promote the community and the arts."

The success and growth of the group, along with the support from the Hermans, and the popular response from the community, has led the group into production of a second CD.

Ron Jolly is a local talk radio host in Traverse City and he recognizes Horizon Books as a third place. He features a weekly segment highlighting the activities of Horizon Books and he announces the local bestsellers. He also features local and regional authors on his show and is an avid customer. He says: "Horizon has the local flavor that only an independently owned store can offer. I know the staff by name, and I can go and meet my neighbors there. It's the kind of place that makes a community unique."

Jim Porter meets his best friend there at least once a week for lunch. Porter is a water quality engineer who moved to the area twenty-five years ago, and is concerned about the downtown stores and the big businesses selling against the independent retailers. "I feel a lot of pride in the store," he says. "It's like the library. I visit there at least two or three times a week." For him, it is much more than a bookstore. He tells the astonishing story about the time he was looking for a particular book. He went to Horizon and was getting some help from one of the clerks who disappeared to fetch it from the shelf. She was gone the longest time and just about when he was ready to give up, thinking she had forgotten him, she reappeared. Finding that the book was out of stock and had gone out of print, she told him that she had called the local library, located a copy there, and reserved it for him. "Will you be going to the library soon, or do you want me to go and pick it up for you?" she asked.

Perhaps the most touching in the entire Horizon Books lexicon of third place stories is the poignant story of a customer we'll call Robert.

Robert was a regular customer for over ten years before his real story was revealed to the Horizon Books staff. This friendly and likeable fellow was known to all the staff and many of the customers by name. His regular visits and wide selection of science, music, and philosophy titles indicated that he was an urbane and cosmopolitan citizen with a wide range of interests. At one point, he even described his efforts in composing a concerto in honor of one of the staff members at Horizon Books.

No one actually remembers how or when the Horizon Books staff came to realize that Robert was actually a patient at the local state mental hospital. It may have been when his father, a businessman living in another city, approached Vic and asked him to limit Robert's daily book purchases and help manage Robert's expenditures. While Robert was marginally functional in society and had what seemed to be a photographic memory, he had been diagnosed as delusional and had been admitted as a patient. But he was capable enough to leave the hospital and had the freedom to shop in local stores. Over the next few years, the Horizon Books staff worked closely with Robert to manage his appetite for books and communicate about his condition. The line between Robert's Horizon Books family and his real family blurred over time and without any great effort, the staff became a part of his life.

Then, Robert stopped coming into the store. People began to wonder where he was. Eventually, his sister called Vic and told him that Robert had been diagnosed with cancer and his parents had taken him home to care for him. When Robert died, about a year later, his family sent a large bouquet of flowers to the Hermans and Horizon Books staff, thanking them for being such a significant element in Robert's life.

Never without a sense of who he is and where he is headed, Vic sums up his philosophy in the face of the pressures put upon his business by the trends in retailing and in the book business: "Our culture has been changed significantly by the automobile, allowing people to live far from their communities; and to a lesser extent by zoning laws and building codes that have emptied our downtowns of residents. Apartments above storefronts are now mostly empty because of elevators and other code requirements. Recently, we have seen a reversal of these trends in what has been labeled the New Urbanism movement. I applaud these changes.

I'm more interested in preserving Traverse City as a viable living space where people interact with neighbors and friends than in worrying about what happens in the book business."

Vic Herman claims that the third place aspects of Horizon Books are somehow accidental. Don't believe him.

PHOTO © OLD ST. GEORGE

The Great Hall of Old St. George is host to the Scottish Ceilidh,
one of the many cultural festivals held there each year.

Old St. George

CINCINNATI, OHIO

IN MARCH of 1999, I spent three days in Cincinnati, Ohio, with Larry Bourgeois, during which I toured Old St. George, met with its board of directors, and gave a talk one evening in the library of what had been the friary. I marveled at the facility these folks had acquired and at the variety of people and activities to which the facility played host. In what had been the sanctuary, I saw rows of long tables on which were displayed the fittings and fixtures of dealers and artists catering to those who restore historic structures. On the evening of the following day, the same space was being used by a local musical group and their friends who were listening to their first CD over the state-of-the-art music system that served the great hall. Old St. George is still in the process of becoming, still finding additional ways to meet the community's social and spiritual needs.

Though on a much larger scale, Old St. George reminded me of the big Town Hall in our little community a few states over. It seemed to be used by almost everyone for just about every kind of meeting, formal and informal. A smaller congregation even held worship services there. Whereas our Town Hall catered only to events, Old St. George counts rather heavily on events to defray costs, but is heading in the direction of more sustained use. Only the imagination of the board of directors would seem to limit the community-building uses to which the facility may be put.

PILGRIM'S PLACE

Old St. George is sacred space redefined. The church edifice, the monastery, and the cloistered courtyard that house Old St. George offer a pleasing and elevating haven from the agitations of Cincinnati. The city's finest nineteenth-century artisans created a German medieval ambience by combining stone, tile, marble, stained glass, and hardwood paneling in quiet but massive elegance. A 1928 addition is true to the original architectural style. The architecture derives from a medieval tradition where a church was a hundred times larger and a hundred times more elegant than the shanties and one-story cottages surrounding it. It represented the unity of the collective, their guiding values, and a permanence meant to transcend the generations. Old St. George retains that aura and remains an anchor amid a life that is so fluid and transitory.

From the church's original institutional faith, Roman Catholicism, we have moved to a "small c" catholicism; a far more ecumenical and inclusive place. We are host to a myriad of programs and events that keep Old St. George busy and filled with people, but the heart of our third place lies in the Pilgrim Place coffeehouse. It's located in the original structure, apart from the great hall, in an area we call "Pilgrim Place" in dedication to those who are self-consciously seeking their spiritual way.

The Old St. George Pilgrim's Place coffeehouse is the only espresso bar sacristy I know of in the world. It is a result of my vision and deep desire to open a coffeehouse in an idyllic and expansive sacred setting, and its success is the realization of my fondest dream. I became a serious convert to the coffeehouse movement and began my espresso coffee pilgrimage in the mid-1970s when I heard the prophetic announcement of the visionary founder of the Espresso Society in San Francisco. He proclaimed that "the espresso bars of the '80s and '90s would become what the alcohol bars were in the '50s and '60s," and the seed was planted in my head to create a "pilgrim coffeehouse." In the same vein, while working my way through seminary school, I felt strongly moved to create bookstore coffeehouses that were focused on community and spiritual renewal. That dream eventually took form in the Phoenix Books & Espresso Café, which I helped establish in San Jose, California, in 1984.

In response to the changing spiritual landscape in America in the 1980s, it became clear to me that hospitable gathering places where people shared their lives and spoke openly about brokenness and healing were great good places of the heart and spirit. Many twelve-step meetings embraced coffee as a secular sacrament of their lives together, at a time when coffee was still viewed in traditional church settings as the "wicked brew of infidels."

The desire to create an espresso bar sacristy probably came from my earliest experiences in and around coffeehouses. Traveling in Europe in the early 1960s and being part of the birth of the espresso bar movement in the United States convinced me that these kinds of places might become for my generation a kind of common ground between the bartender and the priest. My gut told me that our culture needed more soul friends in the form of spiritual bartenders and coffeehouse priests.

Though this passionate idea firmly took root in my heart, it was many years before it found a physical home. The first inkling I had that my dream could become a reality was when I moved to Cincinnati ten years ago. The week I arrived in town, I visited a friar in the monastery of St. George. I immediately saw that the principles behind the bookstore coffeehouse I had helped create in California could be used as the foundation for a new kind of spiritual bookstore coffeehouse, and Old St. George would be the perfect setting.

There were two major problems to overcome: First, major institutional religions don't normally hand over management of their cathedrals to independent thinkers, social architects, and spiritual entrepreneurs, which is how I define my vocational track. Second, Old St. George was registered as a major historic property and located immediately adjacent to the University of Cincinnati, which had made it clear that they were interested in using the property to expand their campus.

By what I like to think of as "divine intervention," three years later the Archdiocese decided to merge the St. George parish with another nearby parish and the property was put up for sale. A few visionary leaders wanted to try to save the property and turn it into a community and spiritual center. I joined their effort in 1994 and we were given six months to come up with a mission plan and half a million dollars to purchase Old St. George before the Archdiocese placed it on the open market.

The community wanted to see the building preserved as a historic treasure, so we had public support, and fortunately we were able to arrange bank financing to purchase the building just ahead of the deadline. Our vision to create a great good place for community and spiritual renewal was finally materializing.

Since this was going to be a community center, the challenge in creating the coffeehouse was to establish a comfortable and peaceful setting with the capacity to provide coffee and espresso drink services for anywhere from a casual few to a thousand. The heart of our business plan was to honor each guest, not as a consumer, but as a unique person who was a gift to the community at large. We had two concepts we viewed as the twin focal points for the mission: "Espresso society" focused on the cultural habitat associated with classical coffeehouses, and "espresso guild" focused on the artisans who create the product itself. The espresso machine, choice of coffee, and the rigorous training standards necessary to produce the best possible product were all part of the "espresso guild" charter.

The passion and excellence that Pilgrim Place coffeehouse stands for is inspired by the lifelong work of a few key "founding fathers" of the contemporary espresso movement in North America. The combined vision of Kent Bakke and John Blackwell, co-creators of Seattle's first espresso cart and espresso importing and service company, and Tim O'Connor, founder of the San Francisco area's affiliate Pacific Espresso, are part of the heritage of excellence that has gone into the continued adaptation and evolution of the La Marzocco espresso machine for the American market.

The choice of espresso coffee blends includes three coffees, with Espresso Vivace from Seattle used as the standard for our lattes. I believe that David Schomer, the founder of Espresso Vivace, has set the standard for excellence for lattes in Seattle and throughout the United States Our "espresso guild" trains for the standards that he has set with deep respect for his leadership.

Over the past twenty-two years I, along with Kent Bakke, John Blackwell, Tim O'Connor, and David Schomer, have made many pilgrimages to the Marzocco factory and become part of the Bambi family (a.k.a. Marzocco International). Old St. George is proud to plot a new pathway or "sacred grounds" for spiritual bartending as part of this great tradition of espresso machine and coffeehouse excellence.

IT'S NOT ALL IN THE GROUNDS

Though the Pilgrim's Place coffeehouse is often seen as the heart and soul of Old St. George, there are many other aspects that make it a destination spot for the entire community.

Our location, immediately adjacent to a major university, has encouraged us to offer a place that sharply contrasts with the abundance of smoke-filled, alcohol driven, casual companion watering holes and gaming establishments that surround us. Ours is a uniquely created and purposeful great good place for community and spiritual renewal.

Our vision of community and our outreach extend well beyond the campus, and this enables us to bring together a diverse group of people in an even greater diversity of events and activities.

We are an open mixing place for the general public, but we are strongly committed to bringing together people who may not normally spend time together in the hope that they will become friends, seeking deeper relationships with each other and with the community. A sign I once saw in an old café window proclaimed, "There are no strangers here, just friends who haven't met," and that pretty much captures what we're about.

We support Old St. George mainly through donations and by renting space, the latter accounting for approximately two-thirds of our income. We rent our various spaces for events and we rent office space to over a score of individuals and affiliated organizations. These resident members of our community in turn attract hundreds of regular visitors who take part in meetings and such events as workshops and task force meetings.

Our religious organizations are ecumenical in scope and include several independent congregations who utilize the facilities as an urban congregation and as a university community chapel. A consortium of ecumenical campus ministries serves the university community and multiple organizations specialize in youth ministries, social justice advocacy, peer-counseling services, media ministries, and other student-related programs.

Some of what takes place at Old St. George is religious in its orientation, but much is not. We collaborate on hosting large conferences with universities and other centers of religious learning whose purpose is to remind the ideological marketplace that a deep and sacred reality is present for all of us in our ordinary daily experiences, and we need to make time and space for it if it's to become part of the healing process that we and society must undergo.

Large audiences gather in the great hall—the former sanctuary from which all pews have been removed—for performing arts events, ethnic festivals, musical concerts, private parties, and both corporate and nonprofit fund-raisers. The nation's oldest community symphony performs concerts here, and their individual musicians often take part in a variety of smaller musical performances. The Sierra Club, both local and national chapters, uses the great hall for public forums on environmental matters.

Small group events, most of which meet weekly, range from yoga classes and reading salons to twelve-step groups and cyberspace forums. Associations such as Earth Connection, the Civic Garden Club, Simple Living, and the Vegetarian group work together in our cloistered courtyard to produce herbs and create recipes for our weekly luncheons. We host dinner/film nights where we watch a film that invites introspection and then reflect upon it while breaking bread together.

Old St. George also hosts large theatrical productions, such as the Indian Cultural Council, Shakespeare festivals, International Students, and ethnic festivals. The Scottish Ceilidh, an annual cultural festival that attracts over a thousand people during the course of the day, is a cultural celebration of music, arts, ethnic foods, jesting, and conversation.

MERCHANTS OF CIVILITY

The lines are becoming increasingly difficult to draw between the secular organizations involved in civic restoration, civility movements, and community service volunteerism, and the religious nonprofit organizations. The latter are working to renew educational institutions and public services and bring neighborhood influences, street-smart experience, and deep religious conviction to bear on academic, political, and civic matters.

We see our role in this controversy as that of a "civility merchant." We are an incubator, a habitat, a think tank, and an essential part of a community of caring and resourceful individuals and organizations. We are deeply concerned about the ever-growing sense of normlessness and disconnectedness evident in communities across America, and with the widespread lack of commitment to responsible public service on behalf of the common good.

Our mission is to be the setting for a community of diverse complementary discernment, talent, experience, and vision that can more effectively see and respond to opportunities that are often overlooked individuals with their more limited vision. Our goal is to be a great good place for community and to offer spiritual renewal by providing a dedicated, multipurpose venue for other organizations and individuals with a similar focus. I think we've succeeded admirably.

Chef Joyce Goldstein cooks up something special in her kitchen.

Square One Restaurant

SAN FRANCISCO, CALIFORNIA

MIDWAY OVER the Atlantic Ocean on my way to Frankfurt five years ago, I heard a TV voice say "San Francisco's Square One Restaurant . . ." and looked up to see Joyce Goldstein, owner and head chef, in her kitchen representing one of the city's finest places. It reminded me of the day I met her at Square One. She wanted to cook for me but my schedule did not permit it. How I have regretted missing that treat!

Joyce (she chides me for calling her Ms. Goldstein) knew me through *The Great Good Place,* which she had purchased for all her staff, and which inspired her to pen "The Third Place" for the *San Francisco Focus.* The book also inspired her to greater efforts to make her restaurant a third place. She was well aware of the limitations. Writing me in 1990, she said, " I learned that my dream may be almost impossible in a city of transients and commuters . . . that it is hard to create community where civilization conspires against you." Judging by the volume of repeat customers, however, it would seem that she realized her dream.

After a dozen very successful years of operating Square One, a dozen years of rising at 5:30 A.M., sketching out a menu, hitting the restaurant at 7:15, walking seven miles a day on the job, and putting in ninety-hour weeks, Joyce has moved on to other endeavors. As it took her two full single-spaced typewritten pages to outline those other endeavors, I'll not attempt to relate them. Suffice to say that she has produced several books on cooking, has taught in several prestigious cooking schools, consults widely, and has traveled extensively since 1996 when she gave up Square One.

Given her schedule, I didn't press for a chapter from her. On the other hand, I couldn't imagine not including Square One Restaurant in this collection. She had provided me with personal letters and a well-chosen package of materials sufficient, altogether, to yield a substantial rendering of her remarkable success with a third place restaurant.

*M*ost *restaurants are* not third places nor do they try to be, but there are notable exceptions and Square One was one of them. Like many of the authors in this collection, Joyce Goldstein grew up amid third places and came to count on them in adult life wherever she happened to reside. It is not surprising, then, that she strove to link good food with good company in pleasant surroundings and with a staff well cued to the same goal.

In presenting Square One as an example of a third place eatery, I will treat, in turn, its basic ingredients starting with Joyce Goldstein herself; next, her food, which always commanded the most attention; then the place, the physical structure; and finally, the supporting routines including her staff and their training.

THE PERSON

The shaping of Square One began in Joyce Goldstein's childhood, when the family lived in an apartment building in a lower-middle-class neighborhood in Brooklyn. Community evolved and was maintained in the local delicatessen, in Dubrow's cafeteria, in Roseman's grocery, and in Mr. Silverstein's candy store. On the streets you saw people, she recalls, but in those places you got to know them.

As a young woman, Joyce lived for a time in Rome where she became a café regular. There, she found, everyone talked to everyone else and you got so used to it that you never considered it rude or intrusive. She was hesitant about her command of Italian, but the locals soon discovered she wasn't a tourist and extended full welcome. They talked about everything and out of it came a strong sense of place and community.

Upon her return to the United States, she rejected New York City, which "looked forbidding, cold, and dirty" and settled on San Francisco, where "the bay, the hills, the light, the muted pastel colors, the smells in North Beach were familiar and comforting." Applying what she had learned in Europe, Joyce went looking for her third place and found it in the Caffe Trieste, quickly acquiring a circle of interesting friends. She went not for the coffee but for the conversation " . . . so that I could return home renewed and stimulated—and not by caffeine." Later, upon moving to Berkeley, she found Caffe Med and the incredible variety of people who frequented it and who never failed to leave her "animated and stimulated."

Joyce spent several years teaching cooking and in 1970 she started the California Street Cooking School, San Francisco's first international cooking school. Then, in 1975, she was hired on at Alice Waters's famed Chez Panisse Restaurant in Oakland. Her years there as manager and chef capped a list of impressive credentials and paved the way for her own operation. It was also the experience at Chez Panisse that convinced her that she would not be content until she opened her own restaurant.

In May of 1984, her dream came to life. Square One opened at 190 Pacific at Front, San Francisco. Those who report on the world of restaurants and fine dining knew immediately that Square One was something different. The name itself suggests a difference that Joyce explained as follows: "We were sitting around trying to think of what to call the place, when someone commented that with a restaurant everyday you start fresh at square one. You go into the walk-in refrigerator and see what's there. I looked up and said, that's it, and it was."

But it wasn't the contents of the refrigerator that determined the day's fare. It was Joyce's waking mind each morning as she laid out challenges for herself, opportunities for her to do her "wild things" in the kitchen.

As the critics noted, Joyce's was not the usual operation that starts small with a limited menu and one or two specials. Square One Restaurant boasted thirty-nine tables at the outset and attracted large crowds at both lunch and dinner. It was an enormous gamble and as she later admitted, "I put too much into it to fail."

Though she assembled and trained a first rate staff, Joyce never felt she could take a day off. Her concern, her dedication, and, not least, her boundless energy were the motivating forces behind the enjoyment at Square One.

THE FOOD

In recent years, some of the newer "theme restaurants" have been so preoccupied with ambience and other aspects of the customers' experience that they have forgotten the importance of good food; and they have paid a price for it. At Square One, however, food never lost its preeminence. Joyce's gift to other people is food and her greatest joy came from looking up now and then and watching a table of customers take their first bites. "Suddenly," she recalls, "they stop talking, lean back, and smile." Her reviews were superlative and appeared in all the right organs. She won the *Cooks* magazine award. She was praised by Bryan Miller of the *New York Times*; and by *King Lear's* magazine, *Gourmet*, and *Food & Wine*, and when the critic for *California* magazine visited for his review, he came back the next day for lunch.

Though *The Great Good Place* made Joyce more mindful of the social experience at Square One and of the relationships between staff, customers, and herself, it is clear that she always considered her first obligation to be the kitchen. It is her base, her home ground, her thing. Upon leaving Square One, she accepted numerous teaching and consulting assignments, all of which focus on the taste of food, not sociability.

Joyce is at times hard-pressed to explain her cuisine, particularly to those who insist upon categorizing it as Mediterranean. She loves to travel and when she discovers a worthy dish, she gathers the finest and freshest ingredients and produces it in her own kitchen. She has regularly prepared some of the finest dishes from Brazil, Morocco, Portugal, the Near East, and so on. And lest it be overlooked, she prepares American foods as well as anyone, with one reviewer insisting that her very best meal is that served on the Fourth of July.

Her son Evan, who at a tender age became one of the nation's premiere wine tasters ("My son the sommelier," Joyce calls him) complemented his mother's daily menus by matching them with the most compatible vintner's products. At age twenty-six, this young man became the youngest ever to pass the exam administered by the Court of Master Sommeliers in England. He was one of only eleven Master Sommeliers in the United States. Knowing wine as well as one can and knowing his mother's food as well as anyone but Mother herself, he was able to complement it in the best manner, and usually at very affordable prices.

THE PLACE

The whole of Square One was immaculate. Never have I seen a restaurant to match its cleanliness and order. There were no "off stage" areas to wonder about; even the kitchen was in plain view. The colors were white with blond wood chairs and blond wood trim on long banquettes with light cocoa-colored padding. The floor and ceiling were a soft amber. The styling was modern, simple, tasteful, informal, light, and relaxing. "Pared down chic," one reviewer called it, a tribute to maximum effect secured from a tight budget.

Apart from the main dining area and kitchen, two rooms were added later, both of which may be considered essential to a "full service" restaurant. These were a private dining room and a bar. Both were artistically done and both featured large, exotic murals. The private room was given the ambience of an Italian garden and could accommodate thirty-two for dinner and up to fifty for cocktails.

Suitable private rooms are hard to find. Having "roasted" several retiring colleagues, some of my friends and I sought in vain for the ideal setting. Either the room had the wrong shape, or we couldn't order off the menu, or the noise couldn't be controlled, or it could only be had on Sunday nights. A lectern was never provided. And, for all the business we brought in, we were usually treated as if someone were doing us an enormous favor.

Not so at Square One. The room could be had for all-day business seminars, for lunches, for dinners, for informal gatherings with hors d'oeuvres, whatever. And as to the food, guests could order off the menu or have Chef Joyce prepare dishes especially for them.

The more a restaurant becomes a third place, the more the bar becomes its social hub. The really mature among us may recall the importance of the bar in Jack & Charlie's "Club 21" in New York City when it was still the place to go. The regulars always gravitated toward the barroom and it was there, far more than at the tables, where personalities went on parade. It was at the bar where most of the legends surrounding that once famous hangout for the hoity-toity were begat.

Many restaurants include bars for the same reason that palace theaters featured extensive lobbies upstairs and down. They are "holding areas" where people wait to see the next showing of a movie or to get seated at a dinner table. Many restaurant bars are no more than that. Square One's bar, however, was a place unto itself, not a mere stop on the way to dining. Many who frequented Square One preferred to eat in the bar—more informal, less fuss. This bothered Joyce a little. She intended the whole place to be informal.

All third places have their regulars and the interaction between them adds immensely to the appeal of the place. Joyce told me that the bar was the preferred place of many of the regulars. It was in that room that they first knew each other by face, and eventually by name. There was nothing hurried about the barroom. Customers were free to sit reading a book or talk with one another about the menu, current events, or whatever else interested them.

Rave reviews made Square One a "destination restaurant," attracting a great many out-of-town visitors. This daily invasion of strangers in the main dining area undoubtedly made the barroom all the more appealing for regulars who enjoyed the pleasure of familiar company.

The sophisticated visitor to Square One usually noticed how effectively a heavy customer volume was accommodated. The authors of a guide to the Bay Area's best restaurants, for example, wrote, "We have rarely encountered a restaurant so original and so well run that serves so many people." Four hundred plus meals a day makes for "action and clamor" as one critic put it, and unavoidably so. But the action was more a plus than a minus and for two reasons. First, it was all orchestrated by Chef Joyce, under whose supervision unpleasantness was avoided. Secondly, the acoustics were good.

Controlling sound is essential to all third places and essential to pleasant dining anywhere. If your town is like mine, quiet dining is difficult to find. Americans, I would guess, have an increased tolerance for noise, as most popular eateries are (to me) disturbingly loud. But too quiet is not desirable either. The best places, when full or nearly so, produce a hum of human voices, a soothing babble that provides a backdrop of sounds of our species in their happier moments. Square One produced it.

This is not to suggest that the architecture of Square One was perfect. Tight seating along a long glass wall was the favorite of neither staff nor customers. Those who sat there presented, at least to some, a "forlorn and exposed look." As people attract other people, lots of glass up front is usually a good idea in that a restaurant's popularity can be seen from the outside. A "thin layer" of them, however, should not be jammed against it.

Overall, the critics were positive about the physical structure, its ambience, and the way it accommodated the majority of diners. Overall, it was another "plus" for Square One, along with the lady who orchestrated it all; the incredibly good food and the final plus—the routine.

THE ROUTINE

When I asked Joyce to tell me what Square One had going for it as a third place, she talked about the importance of constants. In several other chapters in this volume, you will find this theme echoed. Return customers want the familiar and the predictable; they like to anticipate a repetition of pleasant times. They also like to be known and greeted warmly.

The first of the important constants was Joyce herself. She was there almost every day and night for twelve years, and she wore many hats in addition to the tall white one. She wrote the newsletter. She wrote the menu. She worked the front desk from time to time, and she was always in the kitchen.

The majority of her wait staff was there for nine to twelve years; the kitchen crew from five to ten. For an operation only a dozen years old, staff tenure like this bespeaks a good work climate and a loyal staff does much to secure loyal customers. All were well trained in the services they performed. One of her young waiters, for example, was described by a reviewer as "an old pro in a young body." The waiter was neither absent when needed, nor bothersome when not needed. So impressed was the reviewer that it occurred to him to include the waiter's name in his write-up, to "make him famous," but the waiter "didn't, bless him, tell us his name."

Reviewers also praised Joyce's thoughtful touches—supplying wine lists for everyone at the table; the ample pours . . . scotch on the rocks as generous as we'd fix at home; the spanking white tablecloths. And then would come the food, "prepared by people who love to cook for people who love to eat" and served, as it should be, with everything just so on white plates.

Though Square One Restaurant's name derived from the fact that Joyce gave no thought to the next day's menu until that day arrived (each day began at square one) there was consistency nonetheless. Wednesday nights featured regional festivals. Regulars with a special fondness for one of Joyce's creations got the courtesy of a phone call when she was planning to prepare it. "It's meant," she said, "to be sort of like Mom making you your favorite food." It's the sort of thing you have to know how to do well if you're going to do it. I once made the mistake of telling a butcher of my fondness for good lamb and got a call every time he got a shipment. I don't like lamb that much.

Joyce told me this: "Places may survive in these wildly competitive times as food and dining establishments because of reasonably good food and financial savvy, but they will not become third places if the 'regular' clientele is bewildered when the face at the door or the face at the bar counter is constantly changing. Along with the chef!"

The social aspects of the dining experience are crucial to the sustained appeal of a restaurant, and the third place vision, as Joyce Goldstein's Square One Restaurant demonstrated, serves well. Many eateries encourage their staff to engage in what is sometimes called "false personalization" as in plunking down a plate of food with the admonition to "Enjoy" or greeting us with, "Hi, my name is Bruce and I'll be your waiter." You may then wait for your three twists from a two-foot-tall pepper mill—that's part of it.

There was none of that at the fine supper clubs along the St. Croix when I was one of their younger customers. There, the hosting was as beautiful as the scenery, but the menu was nothing like that at Square One. Joyce put it all together, and I think about as well as it can be done.

There's pretty good evidence that she did. In 1999, Joyce wrote: "Although Square One has been closed for almost three years I still hear from many of our regular guests, both bar and main dining room, because they miss their third place and have not found a replacement. They still want to keep in touch. I consider this one of the highest compliments paid to Square One and to me."

People gather at El Taco Nazo during a neighborhood event.

El Taco Nazo

POMONA, CALIFORNIA

POMONA IS one of many American cities making a comeback and assisting in its revitalization is streetwise and city hall–wise Peter Apanel who, in an earlier career, did much to foster community in nearby Pasadena by originating the "Pasadena Doo Dah Parade." Pomona's revival has been spearheaded by a "Triple A" approach focusing on academics, antiques, and the arts, a combination with a strong downtown emphasis and one that puts interesting people in the streets.

Peter has always recognized the importance of third place meeting and gathering sites and was involved with Pomona's emerging art colony when Café Taco Nazo burst onto that scene. This café demonstrates the superiority of the local independent establishment over chain operations. Its owner has been responsive to her customers in ways chains never are. Her café's contribution to a unique sense of place in Pomona's art district is already considerable. Particularly in areas devoted to the arts, the shameless spread of banality should find its limits.

Apparently, however, there were those in the local government who would have preferred a "McBurger" to a third place. Increasingly, we encounter planners and other officials who've grown up in areas lacking a robust community life, and it rather alarms some of them. Fortunately, early objections to the character of Café Taco Nazo have been overcome.

For the most part, I'm sure the concept of a third place conjures up the notion of a hangout that's taken a long time to develop. But in the Arts Colony district of downtown Pomona, thirty miles east of downtown Los Angeles, there's a Mexican restaurant called El Taco Nazo that opened for business in January 2000 and instantly became a third place.

The building at the southeast corner of Second and Main that now houses El Taco Nazo was built one year before train service came to Pomona in 1885, and has witnessed the entire history of downtown Pomona, from boom to bust, and now revitalization.

The boom started in the 1880s, and lasted up until the 1950s. Then the freeways and shopping malls changed the economic landscape of the region. In 1962, the city chose a cure for downtown Pomona's ills that turned out to be worse than the disease—a pedestrian mall. And by the mid-1970s, downtown Pomona was practically a ghost town.

But revitalization was not far behind. A newly founded medical college moved into a single storefront in 1977, and today covers more than six square blocks that were once occupied by major department stores, all of which have now been renovated by the college, and converted into classrooms and administrative facilities.

Just to the west, also starting in the late 1970s, antique dealers began moving into an area filled with smaller storefronts. That two-block-long stretch is now fully occupied and officially known as Antique Row.

Farther to the west, however, downtown continued to languish, and it wasn't until the early 1990s that things began to turn around, when a local attorney and his family made a commitment to buy and renovate property, with the intent of creating an arts colony.

Today, the Arts Colony has over a dozen galleries, plus specialty retail shops, restaurants, entertainment venues, and over sixty live/work lofts. Plus, four nearby universities and colleges have opened up satellite facilities, one of which includes a live theater.

But before El Taco Nazo opened, business owners and residents in the Arts Colony could sense that something was missing, even if they couldn't articulate just what it was. And it wasn't until El Taco Nazo opened for business that the Arts Colony finally got the sense of community that had been missing from the revitalization equation.

The Arts Colony is still a relatively new neighborhood in terms of social relationships and shared histories, with most business owners and residents having ties to one another that only go back one or two years. Without the presence of a third place to serve as a social catalyst, the development of the Arts Colony's sense of community had clearly lagged behind the physical revitalization of the area.

It's not as if there weren't other third places already present before El Taco Nazo opened, but the kinds of third places that already existed didn't fill the neighborhood's need for a full-time, neutral, all-purpose, all-ages hangout.

There's a hair salon whose customers and employees often sit out in front, serving as the social hub on that block.

On the next block over, there's a metaphysical shop that has its own group of friends and customers who also sit out front, and serve as the social hub for what has come to be known as "Estrogen Row," because six out of seven businesses on that side of the block are owned by women.

In both cases, the street scenes in front of these third places benefit from having large raised planters, landscaping remnants of the pedestrian mall, situated between very wide sidewalks and a narrow, slow-moving roadway, providing a sense of enclosure that makes the area in front of these storefronts feel like a front porch.

Also, many of these century-old storefronts have been converted into live/work units, so business owners live on the premises and often get together after business hours for barbecues and informal socializing on the sidewalk. And around the corner, every Friday night, one gallery owner hosts "Café George," a potluck dinner that attracts up to twenty-five artists and their friends.

But before El Taco Nazo opened, there had been no place to go at any given time, day or night, seven days a week, for a beer, or to meet with friends, or to just hang out. The nearest neighborhood bar is about three blocks away separated from the Arts Colony by a pedestrian-unfriendly boulevard. And the two restaurants in the Arts Colony that serve espresso drinks don't have long hours on a daily basis throughout the week.

And so, as soon as it opened for business, with good, inexpensive food, beer, pool tables, and a sidewalk patio—open seven days a week, from 9:00 A.M. to 10:00 P.M., and even later on weekends—El Taco Nazo instantly became the third place for the entire neighborhood.

But it wasn't just a matter of being in the right place at the right time with the right idea. Others had tried and failed to create a third place at that same location.

Seven years earlier, the space now occupied by El Taco Nazo had been the attorney's office, and when the attorney moved out, his son enlisted a friend to open a coffeehouse there.

It was the son's idea to create a loss leader to jump-start the neighborhood, and the coffeehouse did just that for the first couple of years. On the strength of personal contacts, and despite the terrible perceptions of downtown that most people had, the attorney's son and his friends began attracting people to this desolate-looking area.

In reality, the area wasn't as desolate as it seemed. There were artists already there, living illegally in storefronts and commercial buildings. And because of that, they had done their best to hide their presence by making their living spaces look abandoned from the outside. Eventually, however, they would serve as pioneers in the revitalization process, and the coffeehouse was their haven in this effort.

The coffeehouse, however, was never economically viable, even with the financial subsidies provided by the attorney and his family. And gradually it even lost its status as the neighborhood's third place when teenagers began to claim the place as their own. The coffeehouse tried playing tapes of Broadway show tunes to drive away the teenagers, but eventually even that stopped working.

So, after four years it closed. By then, however, the neighborhood had started to gain positive attention throughout the area, and the owners of a small deli in another part of town signed a lease to take over the space and convert it into a sports bar with a sit-down restaurant.

But the sports bar never caught on, either financially or as a third place, and by the time El Taco Nazo finally bought the sports bar two and a half years later, a local paper called the location "cursed."

So, what then caused the instant turnaround?

The pool tables, the televisions, the patio, and the beer are still there. The food is much better, but the price range is pretty much the same, and the decor has been changed only slightly. Yet by the second day of business, despite bad weather, no grand opening, and the sports bar's old signs still hanging outside, El Taco Nazo was packed for lunch, and stayed busy all day long. And there was more to this success than simply being busy. It felt like a reunion.

While two local artists were off to one side of the restaurant painting a mural that subtly portrays people from the neighborhood in Mayan-looking imagery, those same people, unaware at the time that they were being depicted in the mural, were popping in and out all day long, going from table to table to socialize with each other as if this had been their hangout for years.

So, if there weren't many quantifiable, physical changes made, why such a big difference?

Clearly there's a vibe at El Taco Nazo now that's just the opposite of the feeling that people got when the place was a sports bar. And the main reason for this is Marisa, the owner, who adds a completely unquantifiable ingredient to the restaurant—she makes people feel like family.

During the month or so between the closing of the sports bar and the opening of El Taco Nazo, Marisa was there every day, getting the place cleaned up, rearranging the kitchen, and meeting with salespeople. The door was always open, and anyone was welcome to walk in off the street and chat with her.

She quickly got to know all of the locals by name. She patiently listened to endless well-meaning suggestions about what to do and what not to do. And she even took requests, gladly making special arrangements to prepare certain dishes not on the regular menu.

So, by the time the restaurant officially opened its doors for business, it already felt like home to everyone in the neighborhood.

It also helped that Marisa hired people like herself, who are just naturally friendly and make everyone feel comfortable. Plus, she purposely bought square tables just so customers can push them together and sit in larger groups.

By its second month of operation, El Taco Nazo had changed the rhythm and pace of the entire neighborhood.

Office workers from outside the downtown business district now drive into the area just to eat there. Attorneys from the courthouse three blocks away walk over at lunchtime to play pool and eat fish tacos alongside construction workers and punk rockers.

Since El Taco Nazo is open later than any other restaurant in the area, people drawn to the downtown area's entertainment venues now have a place to stop in before or after a show, generating more customers for the neighboring specialty shops that stay open late.

Pedestrian traffic has now picked up on weekends, too, and this has encouraged galleries to open on Sundays.

However, even with Taco Nazo's success, Pomona is not immune from having the problems that threaten many third places.

Ask anyone what they want to see happening downtown, and they'll tell you that they want a lively, thriving downtown business district. But too many people will quickly add, "but I don't want . . . " and go on from there to describe some of the most positive attributes of third places.

There were even times when it seemed that some people were actually afraid of seeing El Taco Nazo turn into a third place. For example, El Taco Nazo cannot have a bar counter because the city no longer allows any restaurant to have a bar counter. And at one point the city also attempted to require that additional conditions be specifically attached to El Taco Nazo's beer and wine license from the state—even suggesting that menu prices be raised, and that a hostess be stationed at the front door—with the rationale that this would somehow be in the public's best interest.

Fortunately, those requirements weren't imposed, but that fact that someone tried to impose them shows that getting some people to understand the concept of a third place and support the creation of new ones can still be problematic.

Back in 1997, Bert Stitt, the guru of downtown revitalization in Wisconsin, paid a visit to the Arts Colony in Pomona, and made one comment that still stands out today. He said that for any neighborhood to reach critical mass, there needed to be at least 1,150 people who either live or work there.

As of January 2000, the Arts Colony was finally on the verge of reaching that magical number.

Clearly, despite all odds, when enough people get together, with all of the physical prerequisites in place, good things start to happen. The pace of revitalization gathers momentum, the neighborhood takes on a life of its own, and a third place is born.

Patrons let the good times roll at Tunnicliff's Tavern.

Tunnicliff's Tavern

WASHINGTON, D.C.

LYNNE BREAUX left her native New Orleans for Washington, D.C., in 1984 and four years later purchased Tunnicliff's Tavern, which dates back to the eighteenth century. Her goal, she declared in one of her letters to me, was to "transplant the *joi de vivre* of my native city to this politically correct and paranoid town."

It was my pleasure, a few years later, to introduce Ms. Breaux to Jim Peters, founder of the Responsible Hospitality Institute. One could not find two people more dedicated to the idea of civilizing the city and to the conviction that alcoholic beverages, responsibly purveyed, play a key role in the process.

The nation's capital is currently undergoing a transformation that hints of Paris in her better days. A downtown atmosphere is emerging that Jim Peters hopes will resemble the active and stimulating "café society" of London and Vienna as well as Paris during those cities' finest and most culturally productive years. Ms. Breaux's operation provides a prototype for what many of us hope will be a hospitality capital as well as a political one.

Lynne Breaux was born and bred to the hospitality calling. The combination of parents and grandparents who catered to the public, being a native of "the Big Easy," and having had previous experience in restaurant and hotel management, equipped her well for her mission.

She operates her business, as do all American publicans, under the hypercritical eye of a government infused with what Joseph Gusfield called the "malevolence assumption" regarding the use of alcoholic beverages. Tunnicliff's is situated on the same hill as Congress and the irony that many lawmakers relish her hospitality is not lost upon her. I can only hope that she impresses them as much as she does me.

Tunnicliff's Tavern is a restaurant, bar, patio, and parlor located six blocks from the United States Congress. It is where politicians, poets, and people of all ages, occupations, and cultures converse, commiserate, collaborate, celebrate, satiate, relate, date, mate, appropriate, and oft act in-appropriate! The word *restaurant* is a French derivative of the word *restore*. At Tunnicliff's, we not only restore our customers' strength with food, we nourish their souls with our sense of sociability. Since 1988, I have been blessed to be able to live my dream of owning a special place like Tunnicliff's.

My hospitality career began in 1971 in the deluxe hotel business and the idea of a restaurant serving high-quality food in a casually elegant atmosphere became my goal. Integral to that goal was that my place would be one of remarkable diversity and attire, hospitable and political. Though some days are nightmarish, the knowledge of the service I am providing and the obvious pleasure of my customers gives me great satisfaction.

Conversation, the prime draw of a true third place, is a necessary component of any civilized society. Oral communication provides us with the exchange of ideas, sentiments, or observations. The spoken word affords the release of the internal demons in all of us. Therefore, talk eases fear. To socialize is to partake in a friendly and agreeable interchange. People walk in frowning and almost always leave smiling. As a degreed sociologist, I am in an excellent position to observe the sociometry of relationships between people in a social group. Urbanologist and sociology professor Ray Oldenburg, upon first hearing of my degree, stated, "How wonderful that somebody with a sociology degree has put it to optimal use!"

The aura of conviviality here is, in large part, due to my New Orleans upbringing. My hometown is the birthplace of hospitality in this country. I don't know of anyone who failed to have a good time while visiting the Big Easy. Tunni's usually—no, always—succeeds in loosening the self-importance and posturing of some uptight D.C. types. I have been quoted as saying, "In New Orleans people play too hard, in D.C. people work too hard." Running this place I do both! CoCo Chanel's words echo daily, "Find out what it is you like to do and do it. Work hard, play hard. . . . " Owning a third place evidently runs in my blood—my father, grandparents, and great-grandparents all owned neighborhood corner-grocery-store hangouts.

Tunnicliff's is located opposite historic Eastern Market, which is truly the heart of Capitol Hill. It is a year-round old-fashioned food market, designed in 1873 by the Smithsonian's Renwick Castle's architect, Adolph Cluss, with a weekend Parisian-style craft and flea market. It is very much like the New Orleans French Market. Weekends are especially exciting with bargains galore, delicious foods, and friends greeting friends. Our Eastern Market neighborhood is truly a thriving interstitial community.

Tunnicliff's Tavern originally opened as the Eastern Branch Hotel in 1793, "stabling horses, lodging gentlemen or ladies." The hotel was located at Ninth and Pennsylvania Streets SE, two blocks from the current location. Englishman William Tunnicliff bought the business on December 14, 1796, and became one of the first publicans to serve food and booze to Congress. He and his wife operated it as a hotel and tavern until 1804. John Nicholson, one of the original financiers of Washington D.C., was Mr. Tunnicliff's landlord, and, causing great scandal, was Mrs. Tunnicliff's lover. In 1800, President John Adams and several of his cabinet members spent many nights at their "great good place," Mr. Tunnicliff's hotel.

Throughout history, politicians have frequented Tunnicliff's, making deals in a relaxed, nonpartisan environment. In 1850, Sam Houston and Jefferson Davis requested their senatorial colleagues to meet in "Mr. Tunnicliff's Tavern in the parlor after supper" to discuss a bill on "maintaining flogging in the military." The meeting tradition continues to this day, with Republicans and Democrats interacting while dining and drinking. In a 1997 magazine article, author Christopher Hitchens noted that Tunnicliff's was where " . . . you can recline in the company of delinquent congressional staff members, in a special armchair-and-newspaper-and-music-and-cigar section right off the bar area."

Tunnicliff's is cross-generational, cross-economic, cross-sexual, cross-cultural, and cross-racial. We are at any given time a rainbow coalition—no prejudice allowed. I know firsthand the positive effects we have on our community. We increase the incidences of serendipity for our customers.

Third place aficionados rarely need the classifieds. Regulars and staff walk in, run into long lost or newfound friends, partake of comfortable conversation and, *voila*, a new job, a new relationship, romantic or non, a place to live, etc. All because they turned off the TV and the computer and departed from the social isolation of the individual or the couple. In fact, I'm sure we have more Tunni couples than most of those pressure-filled "single's bars." Third places abate loneliness. Tunni regulars know that a date is not necessary for those dreaded big date occasions. No date for New Year's Eve? No problem. The serendipitous group thing here is healthy and happy, laid back and relaxed.

As a third place, not work, not home, Tunnicliff's possesses a camaraderie-conducive continuity. The daily little vignettes are pleasurable . . . the lusty laughter resonating in the air, the robust and amusing conversations, which are sometimes raunchy, always politically incorrect, and yet so appropriate and healthy for the participants. Plots are hatched and organized: the cleanup of a small, neglected neighborhood park, an annual Tunni golf tournament, fund-raising for numerous causes, a communal push for later Metro hours and increased public safety, and so on. One of our annual charity events is the spring fund-raiser for our local Boys and Girls Club. The kids make beautiful paper flowers that customers purchase and personalize and we use to decorate the restaurant. Suddenly, spring has sprung! The group's former director is part of our staff family and is now a Harvard graduate student.

Holidays and their traditions are greatly anticipated and celebrated at Tunni's. We started the first Hill-o-ween and Holidays on the Hill eleven years ago. They have grown to be wildly popular neighborhood events drawing hundreds of children and adults. For Hill-o-ween, our purveyors donate apple cider and mini-weenies that we give out to the neighborhood trick or treaters. Other local businesses now pitch in and provide a haunted house, pony rides, and hayrides. For our Christmas celebration, Holidays on the Hill, Santa arrives by horse and buggy—no need to go out to a suburban mall. We roast chestnuts—a first for many of the kids, organize caroling, and everyone is in a festive holiday mood. And as with Hill-o-ween, other local businesses pitch in and contribute to the activities. Perhaps our most famous annual celebration is Mardi Gras, our biggest night of the year, wild and crazy, just like Bourbon Street! For Mardi Gras and Hill-o-ween, everyone dons costumes and alter egos, and a fun sense of adventure abounds.

Life's cycles—births, passages, deaths, divorces, sicknesses, and successes—are shared social experiences at Tunnicliff's, benefiting all involved. For a dramatic example, one of our regulars needed two open-heart surgeries. The Tunni family opened their hearts and wallets. Banners were hung announcing a travel-home fund for her recuperation, money poured in. This led to fellow government employees transferring to her months of their unused combined annual leave for her long-term recovery process. She is doing great and is amazed by the gracious giving of time, money, and love at this crisis moment of her life.

Recently, a lovely young Tunni couple gave birth to their first child, a beautiful baby boy, and the next day one of our most beloved regulars died after an arduous battle with cancer. Two weeks before her death, she celebrated her fifty-third birthday here. The joyful yet bittersweet memories will remain with her numerous friends forever. She was our official Hill-o-ween apple-bobbing lady for the past ten years. This year's apple bobbing was dedicated to her in the form of a banner. Life's inevitable beginnings and ending are beneficial for the soul when shared with friends and found family.

One of our local rites of passage is the first time neighborhood kids venture into Tunnicliff's with their peers, sans parents, proudly ordering, paying, and tipping. Many of these same kids end up working here.

The blizzard of 1993 paralyzed the burbs and vitalized Capitol Hill. News reports of suburbanites trapped indoors and of Hillites taking to the streets, skiing, walking, or sledding exemplifies how lucky we are to have walking-distance third places in our neighborhood. NoVaps (Northern Virginia People) were frozen in their homes, transportation-less, with encroaching familial closeness, and most likely, playing with their isolating electronics. Whereas, during those eleven consecutive wonderful snow days, Tunni's was packed and we Blizzard Buddies will never forget the ensuing camaraderie of beating the weather together.

D.C. experienced a power brownout in January of 1995, during which the mayor ordered all nonessential businesses, including restaurants, to close. Customers were calling in a panic to see if we were open, disputing the government's definition of "essential." Capitol Hill taverns stuck together and stayed open, much to the relief of our regulars. So instead of hundreds of individual ovens, heaters, and television sets wasting thermal units, everyone congregated in just a few watering holes, conserving energy and having a ball. Ah, the unwitting irony of government. God and Ray Oldenburg know that we are indeed an essential business.

The interconnectedness between current, past, and future staff and our regulars is amazing. The lines are all blurred. Oftentimes, when regulars are hanging out at the bar with too much time on their hands, they are put to work and find new careers here. These are people who otherwise would never know one another, all wonderful kinds of folks—black, white, gay, straight—all with only one common denominator: respect for each other. Of our twenty or so employees, 50 percent have been here for four to nine years, which is an amazingly low turnover rate for our industry. About 25 percent have been here over a year. The remaining 25 percent constitutes a frustrating revolving door, costly and time consuming. One of the reasons for the overall low turnover is due to our schedule flexibility. Time-off requests are usually granted, because for our customers to be happy, the staff must be as well. Sincere smiles are necessary. Though sometimes, the staff can get a bit too relaxed and need to be reminded that it is, still, work. We try to hire self-motivators who understand Matisse's quote, "It is very difficult to make things look easy."

One of our essential staff members started here as dishwasher at the tender age of fourteen, an inner-city kid with much potential. Now ten years later, he is one of our bartender/managers, a well-trained hospitality professional, proud of his accomplishments. He is also a reservist in the District of Columbia National Guard, through which he nominated me to go on a Bosslift trip. Bosslift is a reward for employers of reservists sponsored by Employer Support of the Guard and Reserve (ESGR). An interesting and informative tour of New Orleans' military bases resulted and my Bosslift report was published in the DC Reserve's publication, *The Capital Guardian.*

As I stated in my report, "Before Bosslift, the reservist's requests for time off were an inconvenience. Après Bosslift, I have an increased awareness of the military in general and renewed respect for reservists in particular. The exposure and publicity have increased our military and professional business. We were recently featured in the *Washington Business Journal* with a full-color photograph and a wonderful accompanying article. Tunnicliff's has become an active recruiter for the Reserves with posters around the bar. This is all the result of the partnering of Tunni's with this very special employee.

While studying for my BA at Louisiana State University, I was shocked to learn that waiters were second from the bottom of the status rung in the United States—only one step above sanitation workers! How horrific to think that serving food and beverage to customers engenders so little respect. Why should it be demeaning to dish out some pleasant hospitality to ensure that people enjoy their leisure time. In France, restaurant servicing is a time-honored, well-paying profession. In this country, hospitality personnel are treated as lowlifes. If I see one more insipid TV sitcom where someone makes the comment, "Did you sleep with the waitress?" I'm going to scream or at least write a letter. Throughout our tenure here, most of the staff have had college degrees, some from very prestigious Ivy League colleges. Yet, considering the low status accorded our industry, it is not surprising that they move on to more respected professions.

Esteemed gastronome and physician Jean Anthelme Brillat-Savarin's apt quotation is also our employee policy statement: "To invite someone to dine with you is to make yourself responsible for their well-being as long as they are under your roof." We take it seriously here. Published in 1825, *The Physiology of Taste* should be read by everyone in the hospitality industry. The good doctor in discussing the first restaurant established in Paris in 1765, states that a restaurateur would be successful, if he/she who practices it "possesses sincerity, order, and skill." He further states that " . . . restaurant keepers have been led by their shrewdness to the solution of a seemingly insoluble problem: how to live well and at the same time moderately and even cheaply." As true in 2000 as it was in 1825. M. F. K. Fisher, Brillat-Savarin's translator and the great American writer of food, wine, ambiance, and France, often writes of her love for him. I feel the same. He had his "great good places" during the reign of Louis XIV and understood their importance to the social fabric of a community.

In Spain, restaurants receive tax breaks for having patios. The officials understand that outdoor dining increases tax revenue but more importantly, it reduces crime. In our country, patios are heavily taxed and discouraged. Our patio is a beacon on an otherwise dark street. Many a time people have run into Tunni's escaping some threatening situation, thus we are a true safe haven. We help improve the public safety of our citizens. Yet, at so many Alcohol Beverage Control meetings, taverns are erroneously viewed as places that *increase* the number of police service calls, whereas we know that we *decrease* crime in our neighborhood.

As owner of Tunnicliff's for the past twelve years, I hesitate to use the term "victory" when describing my "great good place." The business of running a third place is a daily challenge, with pitfalls abounding. The current environment in the United States for hospitality establishments—alcohol-pushers—is hostile, unfriendly, and treacherous. Our leaders seem to forget that Jesus drank wine. Moreover, he was so hospitable that he turned water into wine to keep the festivities going at his friends' wedding. Our societal contributions are obliterated by our government's misguided attacks on our industry.

Hospitality is defined as the kind and generous service of customers. Therefore, true hospitality cannot be separated from responsible hospitality. In addition, just as in Mr. Tunnicliff's time, the healthy political machinations occurring here are quite numerous and satisfying to behold, thus making our government's anti-hospitality stance all the more mystifying and ironic. Despite our government's assumption that any place with alcohol is evil, families and non-drinkers feel comfortable here. As at the Cajun fais-do-do's, all ages interact and have a good time.

To paraphrase Louis Armstrong's song "What a Wonderful World": " . . . I see friends shake hands, sayin' how do you do. They're really sayin', I love you. I see babies cryin', I watch them grow. *What a great, good place we have, of that I know.* . . . " Third places have always played an important role in society and I am proud to continue my publican predecessor's tradition of historic Hill hospitality. As M. F. K. Fisher stated in *As They Were*, " . . . I am among the most blessed of women, still permitted to *choose*," I say, "Ditto."

A meeting of the minds. (l-r) Ray Romar, Alan Cassidy,
Theo Karantsalis, and Peter Michas

Miami Passport Photo Shop

HIALEAH, FLORIDA

"ISN'T THIS what life is all about?" That was the note scrawled beneath a feature Sandra Garcia had written about Theo Karantsalis and his shop for the *Miami Herald* in December of 1999. I then called Theo, who had written the note, and asked him to contribute to this book.

Karantsalis is one of those wonderful proprietors who can run a business and host a bull session in the same place during the same hours. Customers take priority, of course, and the regulars always defer to them, but there is no tension in the mix. Ms. Garcia's feature had little to report about Theo's business; it was the goings-on between the owner and his non-customers that had human interest. "Like a bunch of schoolboys," she wrote, "they engage in philosophical debate, discuss the topics of the day, and break into friendly bickering." To put it another way, they all have black belts in the art of hanging out.

We see in Theo's Passport Photo Shop a vestige of the ancient Greek wine bars in which small groups gathered and in which men, in conversation, established unique identities as they injected their views on the widest variety of subjects. Those who give themselves to this camaraderie come to realize that each party to it is a "oner," a truly unique human being, and that knowing such individuals is one of the blessings of being alive.

It's not every day that you come across a place like the Miami Passport Photo Shop. We are a rare kind of third place in that we've managed to re-create a classroom of sorts, a place where each participant is an integral part of the group and is drawn here in search of an experience. Though we are proud to consider ourselves a great good place to a multitude of people, the core group consists of five men, including myself, whose occupations range from retired Exxon executive to physicist/musician to computer software engineer. We aim to do something that most folks in this society choose not to do these days: think.

Our conversational fodder comes from a variety of sources, though our group is deeply grounded in the ideas and literature of Athens and Rome. Everyone should know that all subjects that challenge the resources and thought processes of the human mind lie in paper vaults left to us by our ancient Greek and Roman friends, just waiting to be discovered. We are the secret samplers of that which flows from these classic fountains. Our goal is to conserve civilization. We welcome any and all intellectual skirmishes. There aren't too many people who can get the better of the guys here in a battle of wits. We settle for little recognition and we don't covet academic degrees, although we could probably wallpaper our office with those earned by each member of our group. We engage ourselves in books of the Western world and consider most books written after 1850 a waste of time.

We tend to take a global approach in our discussions by subscribing to periodicals that span myriad boundaries. For example, we subscribe to *State* (Department of State), *Competitive Intelligence,* and the *Investors Business Daily.* The Web site Stratfor.com offers an interesting train of thought on world events, and our periodic issue of *Intelligence and National Security* from Frank Cass in London ensures that we will get our chance to analyze just who is calling the tune, and who is dancing, in the world of government intelligence, foreign policy, and national security today. We are trying to find out just what makes people think and act the way they do. There is always a discussion waiting to happen. Some of us are eccentric and quarrelsome, but also learned and innovative in the field of thought and discovery.

We also stock up on books. Frederick Douglass once said that a man is truly free only when he has learned to read. It stimulates the mind. I bought fifty copies of Norton's *Anthology of World Masterpieces* (on sale), and passed them out to the group. We have been discussing some of the stories for over a year now. Ray, another member of our regular crew, wrote a detailed book on physics and mathematics. Although I think I may be the only person who bought a copy, it is evidence that our group tends to think inventively and take intellectual risks. Our third place cultivates the opposite of agreement and insists instead on argument and debate. Dissent is prized in our forum and every statement is subject to a disciplined process of doubtful questioning.

CULTIVATING THE ESSENTIALS

Our thoughts and conversations have also involved deep reflection on and analysis of our special place, and we've discovered certain important elements necessary to the creation of an environment worthy of being called a third place. For instance, you must be completely open and sincerely interested in what others have to say. Each of us has an innate ability to ferret out deception. A friendly smile is the bond that holds our group together. Set the proper tone, and understand that each participant shares the space. The appearance means very little, but if your place is too sterile, it might work to stifle the experience that you're trying to create. The setting should be relaxed and open to all who accept the challenge to swim defiantly against today's tide of censorship. We share a comfortable sofa left as garbage in an alley, and it serves just fine. You want to be able to plop down on something and not have to worry about staining it. You probably have a friend or relative who has a see-through plastic cover on their sofa at home. This is not inviting. An ATP (anti–third place) maneuver would be akin to what Admiral Hyman Rickover of the U.S. Navy did when he had an inch cut off of the two front legs of the chairs in his office. The visitors kept sliding off, and ultimately got the hint that it was time to leave. Be sure to eliminate all barriers. Plastic chairs, milk crates, and other improvisations can always serve to make an environment look inviting. Be creative.

It's OK to be without the latest electronic gadgetry. The other day, a beeping noise sounded on the University of Miami campus, and everyone reached for their sides—the way one would reach for a six-shooter in the wild west—to answer a most annoying, ubiquitous, and probably unimportant phone call. Our technology-based society has changed the way we work, live, and communicate. A low-tech, unpretentious, and even plain location is ideal for a third place. Clocks and watches mean little in a third place. Most third placers have something that a majority of folks lack today: time.

Develop your ability to make small talk. It's a skill that will help expand your social networking. Don't be afraid to start a conversation. Show some chutzpah. Don't just sit there. Argue! The element of surprise will also help keep you on your toes. Everyone must have a chance to stand on his soapbox. If sometimes you feel foolish or rejected, then you're doing just fine. If you talk too much, someone will surely interrupt and the conversation will evolve and take a new direction.

Humor increases rapport, and certain trigger words can stimulate a conversation. Pete's statement that "most people try to make money the old-fashioned way—they steal it" stirred our group up into a frenzy that lasted about six months. We discussed usury through the ages, the Rothschilds, and the world banking system in detail.

It is critical to be an independent thinker. Unlike most analysts on Wall Street, the folks in third place settings are not bought and paid for, so they say what they really feel. You can't get fired by your comrades, but you can be verbally chastised. A perfect metaphor would be to hold a rubber band taut between two hands. You can pull it in any direction, but when you let it go, it always snaps back. The gang works like a rubber band; they will always keep you from going too far in any direction. Think about a time in your life when someone said something with such profundity that you were awestruck. Consider the scene in the Bible when Jesus Christ stated, "Father, forgive them, for they do not know what they do" and was subsequently resurrected, our entire world changed forever as many embraced Christianity. Words can have a life-changing effect on one's thought processes and views on life. Be independent and oppose the crowd.

What draws people to the Miami Passport Photo Shop is the idea that we are working together toward a single, all-consuming ideal—a commitment without reservation to understanding our fellow man. Without a true mission and substance, there can be no third place. We are searching for answers to serious questions. For example, why do we watch sporting events but refuse to participate in them? We listen to music but do not play any instruments. We buy nice homes but hire others to decorate them. We allow the media and advertising to dictate what we should buy and consider tasteful. We vociferously question the actions of our politicians but fail to vote. A third place offers a forum where we can debate these kinds of questions, and searching for the answers is absolutely vital to the production of the kind of citizens necessary for America's continued safety and happiness.

Creativity is another key element of a third place, and it begins with our attitudes. We are constantly analyzing and searching for solutions to the world's problems. Stop and think about what is really important in your life. Those who achieve the most usually enjoy themselves the most. They understand that this is the best way to create something of lasting value. Third place interactions are highly valuable, and everyone should set aside time to enjoy them. It is a think tank where ideas are shared. Here is a sample thought: Our friend Alan brought up the fact that today's modern home boasts more rooms, walk-in closets, and bigger garages than those built fifty years ago. But today's families are much smaller. Pete built on Alan's thought by stating that today's husband and wife both work, and wonders why. Pete said that it is because society has told today's family that a voracious appetite is good. We all agree on the problem but are never satisfied with the answers and continue to look in new directions.

Although the topic constantly changes in a great good place, the sense of belonging never does. You can get married, divorced, or change jobs, but your place in your third place will always remain intact. You will develop close, personal relationships different from any you have ever experienced before. Part of this comes from actively listening to your comrades. In the beginning stages of creating your third place setting, it is imperative to communicate with others. Always assume that what the other person has to say is important, regardless of their appearance. Many of us are taught at an early age to discount what others have to say if they aren't dressed appropriately.

A company president or well-dressed individual cannot pull rank in our shop. Perhaps this is refreshing to some of our clientele, which include high-ranking government officials and visiting attachés. Their positions mean little to us, and they must admire the fact that we tell it like it is. Everyone is on the same level, and if you try to pull rank, you will most certainly be knocked down a few pegs. A medical doctor is treated the same as a street person, and everyone will eventually end up being the butt of a joke, a hero, or a villain, depending on the tempo of the group. The mood can change like the wind, but by the next day, the chalkboard is wiped clean. We try to probe deep into the psyche of everyone who visits the shop to discover, among other things, the effects of advertising, the media, and other stimuli on the person. Many people have talked about the American way of life, but not many have asked themselves what this means. The best way to understand our culture is to honestly observe several indexes. Indexes such as the types of stimulation one responds to are usually the most revealing. Emerson once said, "If we encounter a man of rare intellect, we should ask him what books he reads." What types of things does the person you're trying to get to know read? Does he like music? Watch television? How often do we stop to consider the "whys" behind people's thoughts and actions? In the shop today, our discussion revolved around the reasoning behind a customer's decision to shave his head in order to gain free admission to a Florida Marlins baseball game. It's important to try to understand what motivates people to act.

You are actively listening when you evaluate the logic behind an argument, paraphrase what you have heard, and focus on the idea being presented. Maintaining eye contact, facing the speaker, and nodding may encourage a less vocal person to open up. The listener is usually in the driver's seat. He can decide where to take the conversation.

Be selfish. Remind yourself that you are actively listening to a conversation to learn something. Thinking and listening can be hard work. When you are done listening, you may offer feedback but only if you have something valuable to say. You may not always agree, but remember that arguing is actually quite complimentary. It means that you were listening.

In a third place, a boring speaker runs the risk of getting cut off in midstream. The group acts like a market of sorts, and has the ability to correct at any given time, and for no apparent reason. The audience is not a group of students on a college campus; ergo, they don't have to stand still and listen to everything you say. As in a court of law, you must be able to defend what you say. You are constantly presenting evidence that will be challenged. Inconsistencies, exaggerations, and misrepresentations will be judged by the listeners. Try to suspend casting judgment until it is your turn to speak. Heated discussions allow one to feel important, but most of all, it offers you and your buddies a way to better understand each other.

The energy, enthusiasm, and creativity found here are fueled by the fundamental belief in what we do. Never allow yourself to compromise your values. Consider the other person's point of view, as well as his or her thoughts, ideas, and heartfelt communication. Before answering, try to develop a well-reasoned position, and bridge the gap between your position and that of the other person. Always use facts, reason, and fairness.

Our lives require a harmonious balance between work, home, and social life. A third place is about cultivating close friendships with a few happy friends in a social setting. If you study and follow the thoughts that I have outlined above, I guarantee that you will be well on your way to creating a wonderfully charming and warm third place. We consider our third place a sanctuary and haven of protection and comfort in today's world. Our goal is to have fun through learning and living. We realize that we can't change the world from our little third place in Miami, but take heart in the belief that we can make a small contribution by presenting society with at least one improved unit: Our group. Each day we close up shop content in the knowledge that there is no greater gift that one can bestow upon our fellow man than that of understanding him.

Ray Oldenburg (center) having his weekly "coffee with the cops"
at the Good Neighbor Coffee House.

Good Neighbor Coffee House

PENSACOLA, FLORIDA

A STARBUCKS employee visited the Good Neighbor coffeehouse one day and proceeded to instruct one of the owners as to the error of their ways. The chairs were too comfortable, they wasted too much time talking with customers, some of their food wasn't fast enough, etc. Apparently they didn't learn, for the very day I picked up Steve Spracklen's manuscript he asked me about the chairs in what has evolved into the library/dining room in our house. We have a colorful variety of heavy, spring-cushioned arm-chairs, most of which began their service in law offices. In them one can spend three hours from soup to cigars and remain quite comfortable. Steve and Tracey would like to acquire some so that their customers might enjoy more comfort than they already do.

Welcome to Hospitality by Chon and Sparrowe includes a type of hospitality establishment they call "Neighborhood/Third Places" which would certainly include the Good Neighbor. In their description, these authors point to "social and cultural dimensions of hospitality often overlooked by those who see only its 'business' aspects." These dimensions are not overlooked at the Good Neighbor and, like Joyce Goldstein whom I've cited elsewhere in this volume, I am more rejuvenated by the good company than the good coffee. And the best of this company is met in Steve and Tracey, our hosts. If you're ever in my town, take Garden Street west until you see that charming little building on the corner and the Good Neighbor sign that has never been more fitting.

In 1993, my wife, Tracey, and I decided to open a coffeehouse. A friend and former business associate of ours, Pat Wingerter, had opened one of the first of the new generation of coffeehouses, True Brew

Coffee, in New Orleans, where we were living at the time. Pat agreed to be our business consultant and get us up and running in our operation.

In a talk about coffeehouse theory one day, Pat suggested that we needed to get our hands on a book called *The Great Good Place*. He pointed around his own coffeehouse, where we were meeting, to two New Orleans policemen taking a break at one table, a student doing homework at another, and a businessman in a discussion with another businessman at yet another table. Pat explained to us briefly the idea behind third places. He said that one of the principal points about a third place was that people were made to feel comfortable doing precisely what is considered undesirable behavior by the mainstream of the fast food culture.

The modern concept in food service tends toward maximizing profits by minimizing the customer's experience in your place of business. The basic idea seems to be: get the customers in, charge them, serve them (or better yet let them serve themselves), and the sooner their backsides disappear out of the door, the better. The drive-through window embodies this principle. The whole day's business can be done in this fashion without anyone working in the place of business either knowing or caring who the customers are. Pat impressed upon us the importance of seeing that customers actually feel at home in your establishment. His advice was, "If you get this idea, you can be successful in the coffeehouse business."

We looked around and did locate a copy of "the book," which should be much easier to find as a modern standard work on urbanology. We both read it, and our coffeehouse concept changed from vaguely institutional to more of a homey, relaxed atmosphere. We had never really contemplated opening a "fast food" type coffeehouse, such as those found in heavy traffic areas in a mall or airport, and which may be contained within the bounds of a kiosk. We did not plan on serving all of our drinks whether or not the patron appeared to need the beverage to go. We weren't thinking of the sort of establishment where the furnishings, if any, are of the type that actually discourage consuming the purchase on the premises. However, in this day and age, with most of the coffee operations that we observed pumping out coffee to go, we had not, on the other hand, considered the establishment to be a third place as defined in *The Great Good Place*.

Another concept we had not really thought about was the relatively common practice in years past of shopkeepers living on the premises of their business, as was discussed in Dr. Oldenburg's book. We had a two-year-old daughter and in opening a small business had to think about how to care for her and run the business at the same time. We said to ourselves Topeka! or rather, Eureka! This would solve the problem of caring for our daughter while running the business.

We set out to find a shop space with living quarters above or behind it. This notion completely bewildered real estate agents all along the eastern seaboard where we first looked for a location. There were agents who handled commercial property, and agents who handled residential property, but "never the twain shall meet," in a manner of speaking. They showed us strip mall locations, huge restaurant buildings, mall spots, but absolutely nothing that corresponded to the building specifications that we were seeking. This has apparently disappeared from the realtor's bag of goodies. They don't even know what it is. ("Is it commercial or is it residential? It can't possibly be both.")

The location we eventually found was definitely not conducive to the fast food type of operation. We couldn't have installed a drive-through window even if we had wanted to. (One of our business consultants told us that this particular convenience was absolutely mandatory to a food service business these days.) Customers would be obliged to come inside to get their coffee. We were a freestanding building, and not in a strip mall or shopping center. We were a room, not a kiosk. We did not go for the great pass-through business we could have gone for in other locations. We were also in a downtown neighborhood, which, by this time, was important to us in keeping with the idea of the business we had in mind.

Our building had been a business called the Good Neighbor Shop since it was constructed in 1950. The commercial part we were going to use as a coffeehouse is attached to a house constructed at the turn of the last century, which used to be a big part of the Good Neighbor Shop before the days of strict ADA (Americans with Disabilities Act) requirements for commercial properties.

The original Good Neighbor Shop had been the first bookstore in Pensacola, Florida. It had grown from selling mostly books to carrying lamps and lamp parts, gifts, a bridal registry, and looking like a magnif-icent jumble. Two sisters, Miss Hazel and Miss Clothilde Lindsey, ran it from the 1940s through the 1970s. We never had the opportunity to meet the sisters Lindsey, but have grown to know them by the many fond and usually amusing remembrances of Pensacolians who share memo-ries of the shop in its bookstore and gift shop days. "Eccentric" and "pix-ilated" are just two of many terms used to describe them. They had def-initely left their mark on our community.

Tracey and I had some imaginative names thought up for our opera-tion when we settled on opening our business in Pensacola. The front-runner at the time was "The Brew Angel's Coffeehouse." With the world-famous Blue Angels flight team having their home base at the Naval Air Station in our town, we thought this would work well. But as we real-ized when we described where we were opening our business to various people in the town, the standard response was, "Oh, you mean the old Good Neighbor Shop." Eventually we saw that we would be crazy to try to change something that was so thoroughly, and fortunately, ingrained in the minds of the local residents.

We began thinking of how we could create an atmosphere that would make people feel at home. We purposely kept the room open and light. Everyone can see everyone else. For furnishings we felt that mismatched wooden tables and chairs gave more of a casual, friendly ambience than insti-tutional restaurant seating would. Furniture with backs on the seats rather than stools would help encourage customers to linger over their coffee.

As to decor, I had been accumulating treasures (junk) through the years of being on the road as a musician, with the notion of opening a saloon someday. A lot of the stuff would best be considered "conversa-tion pieces," as they were commonplace enough articles in their time, but are rare to see now.

What we opened, by virtue of its location, would have to be more of a destination than a stop on the way to a destination. I believe this has prob-ably cut our impulse coffee sales in half, at the very least, with today's rushed life. That is the debit side of the ledger. On the plus side, we have some of the most loyal patrons in the world, and have met some really great people who have gravitated to our business because of what we represent.

Many of the people who come in regularly have become friends with other regulars, who are there solely because they can spend time there, converse, swap ideas and opinions, share shopping tips, brag about accomplishments, catch up on gossip and news, give gratuitous advice, and, oh yes, have a great cup of coffee. Conversations do not have an expiration time based on hours. They are left at one point or another one day to be picked up and continued the next day or next week. We have some conversations that have been in progress for years.

As for ourselves, we are never at a loss for advice on goods and services in our area, or the latest in political, community, and social tidbits. We have found a great place to buy a car, the most reliable repair services in the town, the freshest produce, advice and tips on how to do various home projects, and an unbelievable variety of useful and useless information on a wide variety of subjects, all from interacting personally with people we see regularly in our shop.

The customers have become a sort of extended family, and, as with any family, some of the people you end up with will not be your choice of who you want to spend time with. However, you have them, just as you had the cousin that nobody in the family wanted to play with when you were all growing up, or the overly opinionated aunt, or know-it-all brother-in-law. These become characters that you wait for with a perverse anticipation.

Although we were new to the area in which we opened our business, and knew literally no one in the town, we made several friends through the business that we associate with outside of business hours. Tracey's two best friends in town were customers at our coffeehouse when she met them initially. One is a minister and the other is a psychological therapist.

One of the best surprises we had was to discover that the author of the book *The Great Good Place*, Dr. Ray Oldenburg, lived and taught in the town we had settled in. One of our customers was his student at the University of West Florida, and when Dr. Oldenburg covered the material about third places in a course, our friend told him he had a place like that, and told him about our coffeehouse. Dr. Oldenburg actually came to our coffeehouse and has been a welcome Friday morning visitor since then. We were thrilled to make his acquaintance. My wife and I highly value not only the direction we got from his book but his friendship.

Among those who have been regular patrons, we have hosted several classes of naval aviators as they studied for their wings and eventually went flying away. One of these was such a regular that, when she got rolled out of the flight program temporarily with ear damage from the training, she became our first outside employee in her spare time.

We have local businesspeople who use our coffeehouse as their casual office for meetings and conferences with clients. Real estate deals, school board planning, dream interpretation sessions, antique car club meetings, family reunions, poetry readings, insurance and legal conferences, and bridal and baby showers have all taken place in our shop, sometimes simultaneously.

The Pensacola police department has offered strong support to us as independent small businesspeople. Tracey even got recruited into the Pensacola Citizens' Police Academy as a result of a discussion about third places she got into with a group from the police department who were meeting in our shop, laying out the curriculum for the citizens' police course.

Our coffeehouse received a free plug from rock music icons Jimmy Page and Robert Plant during their concert in our town, when, in talking about things they had enjoyed in our town, they referred to our business as the "quaint coffeehouse on Garden Street." Nobody in the shop had even recognized them when they came in.

We were interested in finding out some of the history of the residence part of our building and learned that the accountant for a local lumber company built it around 1900. All we could find in the records was that the family's name was Fox. We had been unable to get further with our research. It happened that a group of French language lovers met regularly in our coffeehouse, and in the course of conversation one of the members of the group told my wife that her mother had been born in our house. She was one of the Fox family. We got her and her sisters to come and tell us their recollections of the house and the family history. They also provided us with terrific photos of the house when it was new.

One of our older regular customers is the spitting image of the late George Burns. When people do a double take he explains that he is George Burns's older brother. He is a very spry octogenarian who still works as an insurance broker and as a justice of the peace. His schedule could tire out a man half his age. Some days he performs up to three marriages in different locations around the city, which can and do include the beach and the prison.

We see all ages of customers, including young parents with their children who come in because we welcome their business and try to make a relaxing family experience possible. In short, the coffeehouse has become an extension of our lives and ourselves. Nothing suits us more than knowing our customers by name and having them adopt our place as a home away from home, their office away from the office, or their official third place.

Diners enjoy the food and ambiance in the main dining room of Galatoire's.

Proprietor Papa Joe Glasper often tends bar at Joe's Cozy Corner.

Joe's Cozy Corner and Galatoire's

NEW ORLEANS, LOUISIANA

I MET Richard Sexton some years ago when he asked me to write an epilogue for his book *Parallel Utopias,* which compared the new communities of Sea Ranch, California, and Seaside, Florida. Richard is an author/photographer who knows New Orleans intimately. His photographic book *Elegance and Decadence* is one of the finest ever produced on The Big Easy.

Richard reports on two very different New Orleans third places. Joe's Cozy Corner is in the Tremé neighborhood of the city, a section that tourists are cautioned to avoid. Joe's third place, as the reader will note, has a civilizing effect upon the neighborhood. The reader is also afforded a glimpse into the social conditions that begat the jazz music tradition.

Galatoire's attracts a very different clientele to a unique New Orleans dining experience. The food is good, as Richard duly notes, but one can find good food all over the city. Galatoire's offers an experience in sociability to which one should become accustomed to fully enjoy. Once the rhythm and routine become familiar and a relationship with your waiter is established, the good times are "locked in." A first-rate third place must be *dependable* and in that respect Galatoire's is always "four-star."

JOE'S COZY CORNER

Joe's Cozy Corner is indeed cozy. The main entrance thrusts you into a narrow barroom with barely enough room to brush by tight clusters of seated patrons. The wall opposite the bar is lined with photographs of New Orleans musicians who have performed there and patrons who have enjoyed good times there. Behind the bar is a neat array of half-pints of a wide assortment of whiskey. The protocol here is that you buy a bottle of whiskey and then order a mixer, typically a bottle of Coke or 7-Up, and with a complimentary glass of ice you are now "set up" for the evening. If a friend shows up later and you want to buy him a drink, you need nothing more than another free glass of ice to assume the heights of civilized bar hospitality. Of course, a bar owner can't make as much money selling liquor this way, but a lot of Joe's customers don't have a lot of money. Joe's policy, coupled with liberal package laws in Louisiana, is accommodating to this economic situation. Anything left in your bottle at the end of the evening can be taken home. Waste not. Want not.

Joe's Cozy Corner is in Tremé, a neighborhood that begins behind the French Quarter and has a more amorphous back edge around North Broad—geographic boundaries that place Joe's near the neighborhood's center. It's an inner-city neighborhood that tourists are cautioned to avoid by hoteliers in the French Quarter. The namesake of Joe's Cozy Corner is Joe Glasper, known as "Papa Joe" by his clientele. He's run the bar for ten years. Before his tenure the place was known as Ruth's Cozy Corner, but it was closed when Papa Joe took an interest in the narrow corner building at Ursulines and North Robertson Streets. The building undoubtedly had an intriguing presence, even in abandonment. Today, under Papa Joe's direction, it surely does.

A broad overhang wraps around the building, shading the sidewalk beneath. Lionel Batiste, a dapper gentleman who plays drums for the Tremé Brass Band, has a shoe shine stand set up in the cool shade of the overhang. At curbside, homemade grills fashioned from oil barrels are chained to street signs. Uncle Lionel, as his friends and clients know him, shines shoes Thursday through Sundays. Food is grilled more or less on Wednesdays, Thursdays, Saturdays, and Sundays, but in actuality whenever the mood strikes. Saturday, however, is the big food day. Patrons bring whatever they have on hand from wild game to red beans. Papa Joe always has something in the freezer. Whatever gets cooked is given away to all comers. As Papa Joe says, "I never charge anything for the food. It's a family thing. Everything at Joe's is a family thing." This attitude is exemplified by two of Joe's "laws" that are posted above the bar: "If someone buys you a drink and you cannot return it, don't accept it." His other law is: "Tend to your business and leave other people's business alone." In the end, both are sage words of advice to help everyone get along amicably.

Joe's Cozy Corner has carved its happening in the historically rich but prototypically troubled Tremé. Diagonally across the street on North Robertson is the meeting hall for the Tremé Sidewalk Steppers, a second-line parading club that marches during Mardi Gras and leads jazz funerals, among other social functions. A short block down Ursulines is a concrete off-ramp serving an elevated expressway that was ramrodded through the neighborhood to the dismay of the powerless residents. At the time they were more focused on basic issues like the right to vote or to sit wherever they wanted on a city bus. Empty and derelict houses are sprinkled throughout the neighborhood, interspersed with well-worn but tidy ones that clearly embody "home."

Historically, Tremé was populated by people of mixed race, the progeny of liaisons between white Creoles and quadroon mistresses. These "Creoles of color," as we identify them today, enjoyed a class status that, although between that of white and black, carried freedom and relative affluence yielding socioeconomic advantages infinitely closer to whites than to black slaves. By the late-nineteenth century the Creoles of color, who were now considered black by the regressive racial definitions of Jim Crow, were migrating to new neighborhoods further out in the 7th Ward. For a brief period, Tremé was a mostly Sicilian working-class neighborhood, as was the adjacent French Quarter. As the Sicilian immigrants assimilated into mainstream "white" New Orleans, they moved out too. Their exodus was plugged beginning early in the twentieth century by Protestant blacks moving to New Orleans from surrounding rural areas in pursuit of better paying urban jobs. The descendants of these black families that have come in during contemporary times, along with a smattering of Creoles of color whose antecedents never left, and a small cadre of middle-class whites experimenting with regentrification, make up Tremé today and form the community for which Joe's Cozy Corner is an anchor.

Joe's reputation is not based exclusively on the conviviality of its cozy bar, sidewalk cookouts, and the camaraderie of Uncle Lionel's shoe shine stand. On weekends and special occasions, there's live music. Musical entertainment is a storied tradition in New Orleans. In Storyville, New Orleans' fabled red-light district, madams would hire musicians to play in the barrooms whose walls were typically graced with lewd photographs of the "girls" who would come down and mingle seductively among the patrons as the sounds of hot jazz flowed out into the street. It was a hedonistic scene that few could resist. In fact, sailors on shore leave met with such mayhem in Storyville that the Navy threatened to close the port unless prostitution was made illegal. So prostitution went underground, as New Orleans jazz music went worldwide. Jazz may have branched out in all directions but its musical roots remain firmly in New Orleans, where today there is hardly a joint in town that subsists without live music.

When Papa Joe took over he immediately took out the pool tables in the back room so that he would have room for the musicians to perform. "Musicians need a place to play," says Papa Joe. "Musicians are what keep New Orleans alive. It has always been a city of noise. In the old days there wasn't a street you could walk down in the French Quarter where you couldn't hear live music being played."

I'll never forget my first trip to hear music at Joe's. It was a languid Sunday evening in September. Kermit Ruffins, one of New Orleans' most popular and engaging musicians, was the headliner, with noted keyboardist Henry Butler sharing the bill. Ruffins was the headliner every Sunday evening at Joe's and one of the grills out on the sidewalk belongs to him. Ruffins is known to enjoy grilling food as much as playing music. It's no accident that his band is named the Barbecue Swingers. Both Ruffins and Butler are big draws at major New Orleans music venues like Tipitina's and House of Blues. Major venues and recording contracts may represent where Kermit Ruffins and Henry Butler have arrived, but Joe's is at the heart of where they came from. The best way to describe the music scene at Joe's is that it's "the real thing."

When we arrived at twilight that Sunday evening, the barroom was already packed. Ruffins wasn't there yet, but Butler had already been performing and was currently taking a break, hobnobbing with the regulars. We made our way from the bar to the club area—a bunch of tables and chairs jam-packed in a room that seemed like it had to be as small as a living room in a suburban home. In the far corner of the room was Henry Butler's electric piano and right behind it the drummer's trap set. It had to be as cozy for the musicians as it was for the bar patrons. There was no stage, no soundman, and no stage lighting. The place was lit up with a couple of beer signs. The rest rooms, the only ones, were at the far end of the room behind the musicians. I was there with my girlfriend Laura and her friend Joni. Besides the three of us, there was a couple who looked rather Nordic and didn't seem to speak English very well. Everyone else was black and from the neighborhood and as friendly as could be. Our presence seemed to be evidence that their neighborhood club had garnered a reputation. People were coming from across town, and perhaps across the globe, to get in on the fun. (Papa Joe, in recognition of the growing popularity of the club, started issuing VIP badges for the regulars to ensure that they can always get in.)

Shortly Henry Butler, who is blind, made his way up to his piano and settled in, joined by his fellow musicians. In no time he had the place rocking. Everyone's troubles had definitely been left on the doorstep and good times were soaring through the narrow corridor of Joe's Cozy Corner. At a table next to us an elderly black lady was dressed in her Sunday best. She looked as though she had come straight over from church and probably had. A middle-aged black woman sauntered up near the stage dressed in a sequined and rayon outfit reminiscent of those that high school baton twirlers wear strutting out ahead of the band. (I presumed she might have been a Baby Doll—a costuming prototype for black women marching with the Zulu Social Aid and Pleasure Club on Mardi Gras Day. I later learned that she was a regular and by day is a schoolteacher, but she likes to dress up when she comes to hear music at Joe's. "She's kind of like a Baby Doll," Papa Joe informed me, "but this is just the thing she does when she comes here. We call her Miss Lolly Pop.") Miss Lolly Pop was brown-bagging a McDonalds's meal and when she accosted a friend at a table near the stage she was treated to a couple of nice slugs of Canadian Club for her McDonalds's Coke. Meanwhile, three feet away, "on stage," Henry Butler's fingers were gliding effortlessly over the keyboard. Periodically patrons dance-stepped their way through the band en route to the rest room, grooving to the music.

As the set rollicked along there was a growing murmur emerging between numbers as the crowd began to wonder when Kermit Ruffins would arrive. Assurances came from Papa Joe that he would be there soon. He was just running a little behind. Late in Henry Butler's set, as if by magic, Kermit Ruffins appeared and began to make his way through the crowd, trumpet in hand. He worked the thick crowd, shaking hands with friends and fellow musicians as Butler's set filled the tiny room with boisterous sound. Kermit eventually made his way to the front of the room, and with his horn poised at his lips, he jumped into the music as naturally and gracefully as though the night's entertainment had been meticulously timed to accommodate his arrival just at that precise point. Ruffins and Butler played together with great bravado and the crowd at Joe's loved it. It was the climax of the evening and before anyone was ready for it to conclude, it was over. Both musicians had other gigs to get to, at more posh venues, where the audience was likely to be exclusively white, and drinks wouldn't be available by the half-pint.

The engaging performance we had just witnessed exemplified a great New Orleans tradition. Casual, impromptu performances by musicians before and after their regular gigs were vital in a multitude of ways to the evolution of contemporary popular music. It was and is important that black musicians, who would have such a profound influence on all popular music forms in the twentieth century, had venues to perform for black audiences, but this was not exclusively a payback exercise. It was important to improvisation. Venues where musicians could interact casually, listen to one another, and learn from one another, together with the benefit of audience reaction to their experimentation, helped drive their music in new directions. Small clubs that offered a hybrid environment somewhere between the highly controlled musical performance of the theater and the audience-less rehearsal hall fundamentally shaped what jazz music would become.

Joe's Cozy Corner is not only a place where musicians perform. It's an integral part of their community—a meeting place. When someone gets a gig and needs other musicians to perform with, they can either be found at Joe's or the word can be put out there. It's common for musicians to rendezvous at Joe's en route to their nightly gigs. Musicians park their cars at Joe's knowing they'll be safe there. As Papa Joe proudly boasts, "I police my corner better than the police can. Everybody has a good time, but I don't put up with any foolishness and I look out for my neighbors."

Joe's Cozy Corner is a vestige of that era in which jazz was born in New Orleans. It represents hope and respite for a neighborhood with no shortage of challenges. Despite contemporary problems, Tremé is steeped in history, a history as diverse as Storyville, the only legally established red-light district in America and perhaps the true birthplace of jazz, and St. Augustine, the first Catholic parish church in America founded specifically for black and mixed race parishioners. St. Louis Number One, the oldest existing cemetery in New Orleans, is also part of that history. So is Joe's Cozy Corner—a neighborhood place where that special environment that cradled jazz is still alive and well today.

GALATOIRE'S

Amid the tawdry landscape of upper Bourbon Street in New Orleans' French Quarter the chance passerby can observe contrasting social rituals. Curbside hawkers lure unwitting tourists into seedy barrooms where the cocktails are laced with Everclear and live nude girls incessantly perform the bump and grind like automatons. In surreal juxtaposition to this hedonism, an orderly cue of well-attired ladies and gentlemen wait amicably to be greeted by the maitre d' at the front door of Galatoire's Restaurant. The dapper suits and elegant dresses of Galatoire's patrons clash abruptly with the T-shirts, shorts, and flip-flops adorning the average tourist. Dining at Galatoire's is one of New Orleans' enduring and endearing traditions. This popular bistro spans the cultural boundaries between the city's Catholic Creoles and its Protestant Anglos, as well as the generational differences within both camps, whose sometimes tense coexistence has long defined the exotic local social landscape.

It is difficult to convey to the uninitiated what is so special about the experience of Galatoire's. The secret, in my view at least, is an abundance of little things that have perpetually resisted change. This resistance to change on the part of both the patrons and the restaurant lends a feeling of absolute security that makes this place as essential as home. The dining room is ample, but not overly grand. It is tightly packed with perfectly set cloth-covered tables. Antique Thonet bentwood chairs grace each table. The tiny white hexagonal ceramic floor tiles are as timeless as the furniture. Mirrors line the walls, reflecting the conviviality of the dining room in all directions. The ceiling is as tightly packed with ceiling fans as the floor is with dining tables. The waiters in their well-pressed tuxedos and starched shirts are as dapper as the patrons. It is all just right.

Galatoire's does not take reservations in the main dining room and until recently there was no waiting area or lounge inside, hence the line on Bourbon Street. Most New Orleanians have a favorite waiter at Galatoire's and ask for him or her by name. I know what you're probably thinking—this is all charming, but rather impractical. What happens when you arrive one day to find that your waiter has moved on? After all, waiting tables is one of those things that college grads do to support themselves for a couple of years while they look for a real job. But this is another of those things that makes Galatoire's special. The waiters are as institutional as the décor. Their demeanor is more like the host at a dinner party than a servant dutifully taking and filling orders. There are menus at Galatoire's, but personally I've never looked at one. Never had to. Certain appetizers, like the souffléd potatoes, always appear by caveat ordered up by the most experienced and vocal members of the party while I am not paying much attention. For the entrée, I always defer to the waiter. After all, he's the host and his advice has always been impeccable. The paneéd soft-shell crab I once had (at my waiter's recommendation, of course) is one of my most memorable culinary experiences ever. But any New Orleanian will tell you it's not the food that makes Galatoire's. Good food abounds all over town. You don't have to go to Galatoire's just for that. Galatoire's is an example of the power of place. It is the setting for ritual. It has a presence as powerful, and as unhip, as the sanctuary of a church, and one is drawn to it like a fish to water. And do not expect a Galatoire's patron to explain this attraction any more readily than a fish can explain its relationship to water. Some things are intuitively essential and are difficult to relate to beyond that. As Louis Armstrong is reputed to have once said in response to a question about the meaning of jazz, "If I have to explain, you won't understand."

Nonlocals who have read about Galatoire's in the likes of *Saveur* magazine go there and frequently don't quite get what the fuss is all about. This only adds to the power of the mystique for the locals who do get it and are confident that their sensibilities are correct. There is not a resident who has been in New Orleans for more than a year or two who doesn't have a Galatoire's story or two in his or her arsenal of memories. My former landlady loves to tell the story of how she was invited to lunch there by a noted Mississippi writer, an old friend of hers, who was in town for a visit. When she arrived, her friend was already at a table working on a stiff cocktail that somehow did not seem to be his first. (At Galatoire's there is a bar at the back of the restaurant, but no bartender. The waiters mix their own drinks and are well known for their strong pours.) An assortment of appetizers began to appear, which my landlady helped herself to, and since it wasn't five P.M. yet, she ordered an iced tea in lieu of a cocktail. As is the tradition at Galatoire's, the food is never ordered all at once, so she was initially completely unconcerned about ordering an entrée. That would all be taken care of in due time. Well, the afternoon drew on as lively conversation was periodically interrupted by the arrival of additional cocktails, which were interspersed with light fare. She munched along, but then panicked when café brulot and dessert was suddenly ordered. It was now midafternoon and the opportunity to more assertively get to the main course had been squandered. So, her tale culminates with, "Well, I learned my lesson, and ended up going home and cooking spaghetti because I was still hungry! So much for being a polite lunch guest."

It is not uncommon, and in fact there is a seemingly subliminal desire, to have lunch *and* dinner at Galatoire's. The luncheon dining experience becomes protracted with conversation, the accretional ordering and consumption of food and drink, followed by coffee and dessert, then aperitifs, and before you know it, it's time for dinner. So, rather than retiring, one begins the food ritual all over again. This practice is known by the adage, "Come for lunch, stay for dinner."

No public place I know of is as inextricably linked to the rituals of sociability, celebration, and (over) indulgence as Galatoire's. Nowhere else is food this good as incidental as this. No one seems ever to have had a "bad experience"—none of the locals anyway. And this is indeed the stuff of legend, which is mostly the stuff of which Galatoire's is made. This is perhaps the true magic ingredient of the place.

A patron relaxes with his late afternoon coffee at Civilization.

Civilization

CLEVELAND, OHIO

I GAVE a presentation at the thirteenth conference of the Specialty Coffee Association of America in Miami Beach and there met Bob Holcepl, whose coffee bar represents the best kind of third place a city can hope for. Whereas chain establishments confine themselves to high-traffic areas and otherwise require the assurance of immediate high customer volume, a place like Bob Holcepl's Civilization struggles through a modest beginning and lean times but, in so doing, plays a pivotal role in bringing deteriorated neighborhoods back to life.

Those initial lean times also mean that the customers will get to know the owners and they will become responsive to one another. This is the advantage of not being able to afford employees at the outset, though it is a dubious one as the hours are long, especially when business is slow.

When a similar place opened a few years ago in a run-down area of New Orleans, those working to restore some of the local dwellings were amazed to see what unlikely people were getting along quite nicely in the area's only gathering spot. Such places indeed civilize a neighborhood and thus Bob and his wife Nancy's place couldn't be more appropriately named.

Civilization is a coffee bar in the European tradition, established in 1990 and located in the historic neighborhood of Tremont in Cleveland, Ohio. Housed in a restored nineteenth-century pharmacy, Civilization is a focal point of daily life for many of the local residents, new and old, in a neighborhood that has undergone much transition in the last ten years. The café was established by my wife, Nancy, and I as a means of revitalizing the neighborhood—and with some hope of providing an income for our family.

Tremont has a long history of being a working-class neighborhood, but over the last few years it has become home to many middle- and upper-middle-class professionals and families and a hotbed of upscale chef-owned restaurants, all of which coexist with long-term residents from a wide range of occupations and income. Cleveland, termed a "comeback city" by many in the press, has a shiny new downtown, but it still lacks essential services in many of its neighborhoods, and only small pockets of the city are considered desirable at this time for new construction and rehabilitation of older homes. Civilization lies in the heart of one of these pockets.

A SHORT HISTORY OF TREMONT

Originally settled in the 1850s, the Tremont neighborhood, because of its proximity to the industrial valley area of Cleveland, quickly became home to waves of Eastern European immigrants seeking work in the nearby steel mills and factories, and grew swiftly from 1890 to 1930 into a densely populated area of the city. The area was so dense that it was standard practice to build two full-sized double homes on a single lot, with a house on the front half of the lot and a matching one behind it, resulting in four or more families living together on one lot.

After World War II, like many other American inner-city neighborhoods, Tremont lost a good deal of its population to the suburbs. Further damage was done to the area by the construction of interstate highways, which divided the neighborhood, cut it off from the rest of the city, and destroyed many of the fine homes along Tremont's main street, West 14th Street. Its large homes, built by early industrialists, made it one of Cleveland's "Millionaire Rows," years back.

Absentee landlords left much of the area's housing stock in disrepair, while the aging homeowner population that remained was marginalized by low-income renters, many of whom were involved in criminal or at least questionable activities. Arson and drugs ravaged the neighborhood in the 1960s. Things had gotten so bad that at one point the national media described the area as the "White South Bronx."

In the late 1970s, early "urban pioneers," many of whom were artists attracted by low-cost housing (average home prices at the time were well under $10,000), proximity to downtown (a mere mile to the central city), and the small-town layout of the neighborhood, began to buy, repair, and renovate houses.

The 1980s brought more new homeowners into the neighborhood, but in spite of this new life, services and retail stores closed or moved elsewhere. Those that remained were mostly convenience stores that sold beer, cheap wine, and cigarettes to those who couldn't get to the super-market located a few miles outside the area. Due to the high crime rate, the stores that remained boarded up their storefronts, which seemed to give the owners a false sense of security. The staying power of the neigh-borhood was in jeopardy. Many new residents, seeing the lack of neces-sary services and meeting places, left within a few years of their arrival.

It was during this time that Nancy and I returned to Tremont. We decided to return because I have long had family ties to the neighbor-hood; my grandparents had settled in Tremont along with thousands of Eastern Europeans in the 1920s seeking a piece of the American Dream, and I was born and spent my early years in the neighborhood. I eventu-ally moved with my family as they followed the trend and moved to the greener pastures of the suburbs in 1954. Upon my return, I purchased a home that was to serve not only as our residence but also as a photo stu-dio, as I was earning my living as a commercial photographer at the time.

Witnessing the decline of retail ventures in Tremont, and troubled by what I viewed as the probable cause of the failure of the revitalization, I began to work with a local development corporation attempting to attract business to the neighborhood. As a "true believer" and as some-one who walked the streets of the neighborhood every day, I could see the change occurring—slowly, but steadily and consistently in the right direction. I knew that Tremont had the potential; we just needed to find someone with enough vision (or at least crazy enough) to dig in and establish a beachhead.

None of the businesses we approached, perhaps fearing for the reputa-tion of Cleveland as a whole as well as our little neighborhood, would, or could, see the potential for any sort of retail business. In retrospect I can understand the source of their fears; a majority of low-income residents, limited access to the greater Cleveland area, and lack of city services would seem to be a huge barrier to establishing any sort of successful retail business in the neighborhood, much less any sort of upscale business.

So, in spite of our best efforts, those early attempts to lure new business to the area failed.

A SIMPLE IDEA IS BORN

After two frustrating years of failing to attract retail business to the neighborhood and feeling a sense of burnout in my career as a photographer, I was ready for change myself. I began to slowly realize that if my theory of revitalization and a bright future for the neighborhood was to indeed to be proven by a visionary (or crazy person), that person would have to be me.

But I still faced one major problem: my funds were extremely limited.

My wife and I had recently renovated a beautiful Queen Anne–style house in the area and we were able to sell it at a small profit. This allowed us to pay our debts, but we still had a little less than five thousand dollars remaining from the sale. That is very little capital to open and operate a new business in a chancy area without proven results by any other merchant and no other income to support our endeavor.

In other words, it was a perfect plan. . . .

What kind of a business should we open in an area that everyone else had snubbed, with limited funds, no other source of operating income, and using a concept that had not yet proven to be successful anywhere in the Cleveland area? How about a European-style coffee bar!

THE BIRTH OF CIVILIZATION

After some false starts, we found a location a half a block from our home (at least we would not have to worry about car payments!): an elegant, though well-worn commercial storefront of about one thousand square feet that had originally served as a pharmacy and later became home to a commercial printer.

The windows were boarded up (as almost all storefronts, occupied or not, in the neighborhood were at the time), the building had been sided over with aluminum in the early 1950s, and the wood floors were ink-stained from years of operating as a print shop. But the building had real beauty on the inside: Eastlake and Arts and Craft cabinets remained along the walls, enough room to create seating for about twenty to twenty-five people, and the original tin ceiling was still intact. It had potential! It was located on a corner one block away from the main thruway and its large windows overlooked a beautiful (though sometimes unruly) city park. Needless to say, we fell in love with the place immediately.

Since it had stood empty for years, the owners were willing to rent it for a modest amount, providing we invested a lot of sweat equity in redoing floors, painting walls, and other general renovations.

Nancy and I worked for months scrubbing woodwork, sanding and staining floors, removing the boards from the windows (not only as a means to invite people in and enhance our business but also as a perfectly practical way of deterring crime by allowing everyone to see into the store), and finally installing the minimal equipment for our new venture. We begged and borrowed everything we could, bought a huge, heavily used cash register, and fluffed the shelves with as much candy, chocolates, coffee, and teas as we could possibly buy. Our entire budget for the renovation, furniture, equipment, and stock was four thousand dollars: literally our life savings at the time! We were broke, but we were open! We even had to borrow one hundred dollars in cash from an aunt for our first days' change drawer.

Our first few months were brutal. No employees, few customers, and little actual experience in the retail food business left us underfunded, overworked, overtired, and over-caffeinated (after all, someone had to drink all that coffee we brewed every day). Undaunted, we took turns standing behind the counter or sitting in the front window reading the paper, doing our best to look like a customer for hours on end without a soul walking through the door.

Our hours were simple; we opened every day at 8:00 A.M. and closed at 8:00 P.M. or when we made at least one hundred dollars in sales, which in some cases required us to be there until late in the evening or until friends, taking pity on us, would come in and buy a few items to help us make our goal. We opened every day except Monday—which we would spend speeding around town in an old van picking up items for the shop. We couldn't get deliveries because we were unable to make the minimum order amount our vendors required for delivery. All our purchases were cash on delivery (or should I say pickup) since credit was out of the question. We had no money in the bank, and the concept of a specialty food store and coffee bar in a poor inner-city neighborhood was not something that inspired confidence in many suppliers.

Thankfully, we began to build a small but loyal following—just a trickle at first, but with some good press we soon became a destination for folks from throughout the region looking for specialty coffee, espresso drinks, teas, and chocolates. We also began to establish ourselves as a crossroads for the neighborhood, unwittingly creating what Dr. Oldenburg describes as a "third place." This was not unintentional, as we did indeed wish to create a common meeting place where neighbors could interact because we thought it an important element in the revitalization of the neighborhood. We just didn't know what it was called. As luck would have it, I discovered The Great Good Place, ironically misfiled in the cooking and food section of the bookshop I was browsing. After quickly reading the book, I realized there was a name for the type of establishment we were building, and I was bolstered by the knowledge I was on the same philosophical track that others had been on for some time. Now we had an even greater mission in addition to restoring a building, creating a business, and helping to revitalize a neighborhood— we were taking part in the resurrection of a form of social interaction that was almost extinct in America.

Within two years of our opening we were able to make all payments to our suppliers and pay our rent and house payments on a regular basis, but we still had little to show for our efforts. We expanded, using money from investors, to a second location in an upper-middle-class suburb of Cleveland. We found that experience to be a disappointment. Our regulars in the suburban café were far more self-absorbed for the most part and the layout and flow of the café left little chance for interaction with the customers in a meaningful way. Our gross income was larger but we found our Tremont store to be a more complete and meaningful experience, not only for our customers, but also for ourselves. After four years of "suburban" retail we sold the unit and returned full time to our first location in Tremont.

In the years that we split our time between stores, the Tremont location continued to grow, continued to produce more income, and, because of our suburban experience, became dearer to us. After the sale of the suburban store we closed the Tremont store for a few weeks and made improvements to the mechanicals of the building, including adding central air-conditioning and improved lighting. We also expanded our menu to include lunch items to better serve our expanding customer base. The larger menu and interior renovations continued to improve our business, and within a few years we purchased the building and began renovations to the exterior, including an historically correct reconstruction of the parts of the building that had been destroyed through the years.

A DAY IN THE LIFE

Our café seats barely twenty-five people inside, plus an additional fifteen seats in front of the café on a wide sidewalk during fair weather. There is no entertainment, no poetry, no angst-filled conversations, no chessboards, no folksingers; we are just a café that serves a pretty good cup of coffee and freshly baked pastries. It is our customers who contribute so much to our allure. Without them we would be just another place.

Being small, we provide an intimate setting; our service counter is only a few feet from most of our customers. Interaction with each customer is natural, and few customers leave without a word or two about their day (or night before).

Every day, beginning at 7:00 A.M., we open our doors to a regular crowd of customers from a wide range of professions and incomes, each with his or her own talent, story, or mission. First to arrive are the white-collar professionals on their way to downtown offices, politicians (including the local councilman), city workers, members of the chamber of commerce, teachers, and construction workers. Some come to sit, while for others we are just a stop on their way to somewhere else. The first hour is barely controlled chaos, as lines form some days out the door, bagels are sliced and toasted, muffins are bagged, and lattes are steamed. Yet Nancy and the staff still remember what all the customers drink and what sort of cookie is their favorite breakfast food, and always take time to trade a few quips and throw a few barbs when required.

By eight, things have become a bit less hectic. There is almost always a table or two of police officers, whether they're Cleveland police, Housing Authority police, sheriff deputies, dressed in plain clothes, or in uniform. A casual customer may wonder, approaching the café, what sort of trouble there is that requires four or five police cars to be present. But the police are friendly, talking with customers, taking tips about suspected drug dealers or minor complaints about barking dogs and unruly neighbors. The police act as part of the community at our café; they are customers, but they are also responsive as police should be—in short they are actually practicing community policing (the policy of getting the police in touch with the community), and it is in practice every morning, noon, and night at Civilization. If there is a non-emergency problem of any kind that requires police attention, the neighborhood residents are more likely to check first at the café before dialing 911.

At a table next to the police, there is usually a local schoolteacher preparing for a day with the kids and savoring her last chance for an "adult moment" for the next several hours. At a table farther down, a local academic sits and mentally prepares for the day at the university across town, lazily reading the morning paper or engaging in conversation with a maintenance worker from the local housing authority about current events or nothing in particular. Having been "introduced by proximity" at the café years ago, they have become friends and meet often for coffee. A small group of laborers ready for the day dressed in jeans and T-shirts gather at another table to discuss politics, union activities, and general gossip.

Most of our early customers are residents, a few of whom work in the neighborhood and start their day with us before "clocking in." What's so special about Civilization is that here, everyone talks to each other, without regard to class, race, income, or profession. Whether it involves people sitting at the same table or two tables talking back and forth across the room, discussions are always lively and interwoven. There are always common topics of concern for the folks to discuss while gathering for coffee. It may be a local issue, it may be a national issue, but everyone has an opinion and no one is afraid to jump into the fray to voice a thought.

By 9:00 A.M. the place has quieted down a bit. A few local artists, writers, and some older neighbors walk in. It is a more relaxed atmosphere; these folks are in no hurry. An older Ukrainian woman from a few doors down, with her little white dog in tow, comes in for a cup of coffee to go, heading to the park as she does every morning. Cabdrivers who ferry kids to the local schools stop by to unwind (one burly driver came in dressed in drag for almost a week and did not get a reaction from the regulars, much to his disappointment I'm sure). An older Eastern European man, dressed in once-stylish polyester, sits at a table next to a minister, chain-smoking while working on a sheet containing betting numbers that no one but he seems to understand. An art columnist from a local weekly publication sits at the bar, drinking her coffee and eating a bagel; she accepts the little performance of daily life at our café as part of her routine. A city animal warden comes in a bit blustery, singing or talking loudly about his cherished native Tennessee team. A local veterinarian might cross paths with the warden on the way to his clinic and have a short discussion with him about a lost dog that they're both trying to help, or he might give some friendly advice at no charge to another one of the customers regarding a pet.

It is a good time, midmorning, when folks are in less of a rush and are able to take a bit more time for conversations, as opposed to the quick banter that characterizes the early-morning rush.

By 10:30 A.M., only a few folks are left; those that work late or sleep late, waiters that come in for their "early-morning" coffee or mochas before facing the lunch hour madness at the local restaurants. Our staff begins to gear up for our own lunch hour, slicing meats and cheeses, washing and cutting vegetables, refilling condiments, and warming the soups of the day.

Lunchtime brings teachers escaping from their classrooms, doctors and nurses taking a break from their rounds at the small hospital around the corner, business folks from downtown squeezing in a meeting while enjoying a panini or wrap, and local artists who come in to talk shop. At this point in the day most folks just come to eat and quickly return to the tasks at hand.

Midafternoon is a lazy time, with customers coming in and sitting for a while, doing work at laptops or paper notebooks, reading the daily newspaper, or chatting idly over coffee. It is a mixed crowd; socially, racially, and economically reflective of the neighborhood.

Around 3:00 P.M., an entirely new shift of safety forces, who are going to report in to work, stop in on their way or right after roll call (one officer told us without his daily white chocolate drink he is much less tolerant to speeders and other minor traffic offenders).

The evening is the slowest part of the day, with only a few folks meeting at the café before they head out to dinner at a local restaurant or to the neighborhood bars. We close early for a coffeehouse—7:00 P.M. on weekdays and 11:00 P.M. on Friday and Saturday. The later hours on the weekends allow us to provide a casual place to talk or have dessert after dinner—without the noise and bustle of a busy restaurant—for those who are not quite ready to return home.

TEN YEARS IN TREMONT

Since our humble beginnings in October of 1990, we have been blessed with many new friends and loyal customers. Realizing in September of 2000 that we had slugged our way though ten years of business, we decided rather spontaneously to have an anniversary party for our store, our staff, and our customers.

We called a few musician friends (including a street organ player visiting from Paris, and a gypsy violinist), rented a tent in case of rain, contacted a caterer, and printed up invitations that were handed out to our customers and family one week before the party.

We were amazed and gratified that afternoon when over four hundred people attended our celebration, overflowing into the street, enjoying each other's company, drinking wine, listening to music, and sharing stories about their experiences at the café. For the first time in a long time, I can truly say that the spirit of community dwells once again in Tremont.

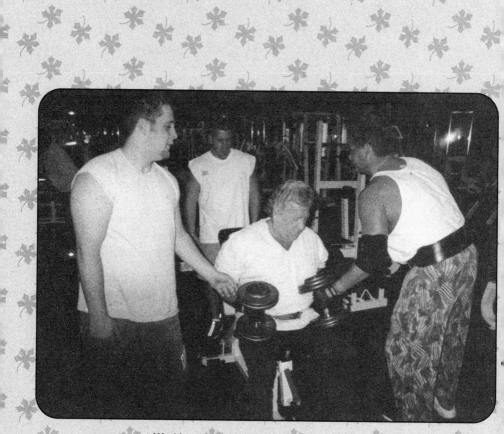
Working out can build muscles and friendships.

The Great Good Gym

ATLANTA, GEORGIA

INCREASING HEALTH consciousness has increased the demand for exercise gymnasiums, and while many believe that state-of-the-art exercise equipment is the only relevant factor in attracting and holding members, the social experience, as Dr. Smith and his colleagues show, cannot be overlooked. From a public-life point of view, it must be recognized, also, that the trend is away from highly visible and highly inclusive third place venues to less visible and less inclusive ones. Translated, this means that more and more people are seeking the third place experience via paid memberships.

A health club has a tremendous potential to become a great good place by welcoming its members and creating a convivial atmosphere. To the extent that this is accomplished, a gym succeeds in providing its members with good health, a beautiful physique, and an improved frame of mind, as well as some very good times.

There are many aspects of a gym that facilitate its becoming a "great good gym," but one stands out above all others: the creation of a friendly, inviting atmosphere. This shouldn't be hard to do, since members usually have many qualities in common and strenuous exercise tends to stimulate common reactions and enhance desirable characteristics. The shared qualities and experiences make it easy for members to talk to, understand, care about, and enjoy each other. However, the usual inhibition and tentativeness of a new member must be dispelled by the friendly approach of the more socially skilled exercisers, initiated on their own or by the staff's influence. The natural processes of developing and sustaining friendships happen mainly between members who exercise regularly in close proximity to one another.

With sufficient friendly interaction, an ordinary gym can become a great good gym. A great good gym is a place where all are welcomed into the fold and mutual understanding, compassion, and supportiveness are evident in the members' interactions. Good humor and good times create a sense of warmth and enjoyment amid the exercise. The gym becomes very important in the members' lives as it helps to sustain their physical health and emotional happiness. Unfortunately, we've found that most gyms do not put in the extra effort required to create a great good place. If only they knew what they are missing out on!

THE GYM EXPERIENCE

At first, the sights and sounds of weights and resistance machines in the exercise facility must surely seem intimidating to the newcomer. The sweat-soaked shirts, the seemingly painful grimaces of those exercising, and the convoluted postures of those entangled in the newest exercise machines are perhaps startling. The sounds of weights clanging, the aerobic machines humming loudly, the rock music blaring, and the members' grunts and groans as they lift and lower heavy weights fuse into a noisy cacophony punctuated occasionally with a resounding "Yes!" as someone masters a previously unliftable weight.

Yet within this world of noise and struggle, a considerable amount of enjoyment can be found, which keeps many members coming back year after year. Both during and after the exercise, many good feelings are generated: the sensation of your muscles working powerfully; the sweaty warmth of your body heated in its exertion; the pumped muscles gorged with blood from being repeatedly tested by the weights; the "rush" as you master increasingly difficult challenges; the relaxation of your body as it winds down from the exercises; and the realization that your body, health, and mind are the better for it.

With experience in the gym, newcomers learn to recognize the discomforts of exercise as signs of power, toughness, and tenacity at mastering physical challenges. They begin to enjoy the moment their muscles strain against resistance, and working out becomes pleasurable. In a comprehensive evaluation of an award-winning gym in California, the biggest reason long-term gym-goers looked forward to exercise was the enjoyment they derived from performing the strenuous exercises themselves.

Between the workouts, there is an ever-increasing satisfaction when their mirrors and scales tell them that their fat is disappearing and muscles are developing. Improvements in their physique soon become apparent in how others look at them. Their energy doubles and triples and they can easily do physical tasks that once sorely tested them. They can feel the difference in their body as it moves smoothly and functions well. They look good and feel great.

But these pleasures are largely confined to the experienced exerciser. For the beginner, the intrinsic enjoyment, weight loss, muscular development, physical improvement, and general good feelings come slowly and with much effort. Consequently, a new fitness member is forced to be satisfied with only increasing strength and fitness, improvements that are obvious only as the amount of weight lifted and aerobic endurance increase. Yet these improvements are often not enough to maintain motivation and a large percentage of newcomers give up after a short period of time.

Many are called to exercise but few are able to maintain the habit. This can be attributed to the length of time it takes to produce changes in physique, the difficulty of learning to enjoy exercise, and the personal isolation new members feel in a gym. Most have received only perfunctory information on how to use the equipment, proper nutrition, and how to develop their own workout routine. It takes a while to learn the best way to exercise, improve, and enjoy it.

New members try to keep busy with their programs but stand around awkwardly between exercises, since the experienced exercisers seldom initiate conversation with them. They feel isolated and alone after being left to their own devices by the staff. For newcomers, and even some experienced members, being in a gym is not a pleasant experience. They don't feel comfortable or at home in the gym. Without a friendly atmosphere that welcomes members into a group of regular fellow exercisers, few new members have the dedication to continue to work out in the isolation that characterizes most gyms.

THE IMPORTANCE OF RELATIONSHIPS IN A GYM

a successful club must offer some added value or enjoyment beyond the equipment and facility. Exercise can often be accomplished less expensively and more conveniently at home or in one's neighborhood. Exercise equipment is inexpensive and widely available. Indeed, by the end of every January, there are numerous people who want to sell their barely touched Christmas exercise gifts at greatly reduced prices. Although club salespeople claim otherwise and naive people initially believe them, complex and faddish exercise equipment are little better than simple barbells and a football track. Exercise videotapes—now available in a wider variety than ever—are also inexpensive and convenient to use at home.

Usually health club management tries to buy new members with expensive advertising and promotions, new equipment, and enhanced facilities. New members join but fade away due to dissatisfaction with results or atmosphere, or a newer gym offering shinier equipment. An enormous amount of thought and money is invested in factors that are of secondary importance in making a gym successful. Social conviviality, the most important factor, is usually ignored altogether.

Most gym-goers, including those who seldom talk with others, exercise at a gym because their motivation and perseverance are sustained and increased by exercising around others, even if they don't talk with them. By their example, the other exercisers provide inspiration, which increases other people's effort and determination. When members do talk to each other and form amicable relationships, they enjoy the gym much more. While management may wish it so, gym-goers do not feel commitment, loyalty, or emotional attachment to facilities or exercise machinery. They bond only to people, whether members or staff. However, it is unusual for the staff to develop relationships with gym-goers beyond mere customer service. The staff almost never tries to facilitate relationships between members.

For newcomers in the usual gym, the social conviviality is the most important aspect of the gym experience because it keeps them returning to exercise and helps them bond to the gym. In the California gym study, the chief element involved in member satisfaction was the positive bonds and close friendly relationships they had with their fellow members. Their positive relationships with the staff also mattered significantly, but to a lesser degree. Positive interactions make new gym-goers feel welcome, comfortable, and at home and help them maintain their exercise schedule. Even after members develop the habit of disciplined exercise, the encouragement and enjoyment provided by their fellow members and the staff still serves to maintain the exercise habit.

WHY IT WORKS

All of us have an innate need to find, enjoy, and maintain enduring relationships with other people we like and respect. The desire for these relationships is obvious in every person's motivations and actions. Much of life is spent with varying success in trying to find a place, friend, loved one, work setting, and group of people with which we feel comfortable, safe, and welcome. At the core of these desired relationships is the desire to feel safe from physical and psychological attack, to be truly accepted for who one is as a person, to be appreciated for one's good qualities, and to be valued as a person in general.

In reviewing their lives, most people will admit that they've suffered the pain of being undervalued, criticized, or rejected many times. Our parents and teachers tried to guide and control our behavior in their effort to mold us into good kids. But all the while, our siblings and peers competed with us for grades, status, popularity, and love, and they did not treat the winner or losers very well. Even in adulthood, we are often judged by unrealistic standards and treated indifferently or negatively by insensitive people. Rather than trying to find qualities in others to like or admire, some look for reasons to feel superior to others.

It's a sad fact that many of us have often been treated as unimportant, unworthy of notice or personal response. While we should all do our best to make our fellow human beings feel welcome, few of us do so, and such friendliness is sorely lacking in most fitness clubs. Most exercisers are treated with the same indifference they routinely encounter with strangers on the street. Perfunctory hellos at the front desk and polite nods to the members are hardly sufficient. Men in particular are relatively guarded and inhibited around others unless they're made to feel welcome.

The gym is one of the few places where anyone can be well received by fellow gym-goers if the person is committed to exercise and willing to be friendly. To make a club successful, the manager need only help facilitate goodwill among the members. With assistance from the staff, members can easily be taught to welcome each other and make each other feel at home. When accomplished to the proper degree, the gym can become a great good gym.

Ultimately, it doesn't take much to make a gym a great good gym. The initiative and assistance of a staff can hasten this development, but it largely depends on socially skilled members. Unfortunately, the staff at most fitness clubs are not astute enough to set the right example for the members. They're usually more attentive to the physical state of the exercisers than to their perceptions and feelings.

A SPECIAL PLACE OF OUR OWN

Every week on Monday, Wednesday, and Friday mornings from 10:00 A.M. to 12:00 P.M., an ordinary gym in Atlanta becomes a great good gym for some of us. During this time, the weight and resistance machine area is filled with several regular exercisers talking and laughing among themselves. There is an easy friendliness extended to anyone interested in joining in, and this friendliness crosses gender, age, racial, and status lines. While we all work out hard, we also enjoy ourselves and the other gym-goers. We constantly move around to different weights and machines and initiate new conversations as we cross paths with each other. Many close friendships have developed from these bright and shining hours in which a poorly managed gym becomes a great good gym.

This creation is really the product of the good hearts and social adeptness of five or so long-term, older members, but it regularly draws in twenty or so additional members of all ages each week. This great good gym, though existing for only a few hours a week, was created wholly by these members, without any involvement from the staff, and the bonds it has engendered are to each other, not to the staff, or the gym. Many gyms never become great good gyms at any time. While it would seem to be the responsibility of the staff to set the stage for a great good place, they too often don't do so. The bonds between members never form due to the lack of spontaneous or staff-stimulated friendliness, as well as the lack of a stable group of members exercising regularly at the same time. But despite our staff's indifference, we have managed to create a place where we feel completely at home, which is the true essence of a great good place.

The current management of our gym has spent millions of dollars improving the facility and the exercise equipment but exhibits a calculated indifference and rudeness toward the exercisers. Only through misguided corporate policy could a staff offend so many current members and drive off so many potential members. Despite the excellent equipment and facility, many gym-goers speak poorly of the gym outside of it and refer interested people to other chains. There is a constant turnover of exercisers as they quit or change to other gyms. Such are the consequences of being insensitive to the needs and desires of your members.

THE BEST OF THE BEST

While few go to the gym chiefly to make friends, the usual gym does work well as a "meet market." Exercisers are generally above-average individuals who mix well with each other after overcoming their initial inhibitions. The opportunities to meet, befriend, and enjoy the company of many good people abound in a gym.

Within the narrow world of an exercise facility, people reveal a great deal about themselves, such as the character traits and values they share in common as well as those they do not. Their character is shown in the self-discipline, toughness, and perseverance they display in meeting the challenge of exercising in order to reach their goals. The way in which people pursue their physical goals at a gym reflects how they deal with the hardships of daily life and the way in which they chase success or try to find love.

Exercising regularly sends a clear message that gym-goers care enough about themselves and their loved ones to make their health and physical fitness a top priority. It also shows that they care about how they look and appeal to others. Having these character traits and values in common makes it much easier to talk to, understand, respect, and like a fellow exerciser.

While gym members share certain characteristics to an increasing degree over time, they are also different in many ways. The gym provides the perfect opportunity to meet a broad array of people we may not ordinarily meet. Exercise bridges age, status, occupational, economic, educational, ethnic, racial, and gender barriers as we work out side by side and share the frustrations, strains, injuries, and triumphs. In our sweaty gym clothes, we are all equal. We are able to appreciate the many fine qualities we have in common and learn to enjoy the differences.

Our lives have become immeasurably richer from working out with a ninety-year-old athlete who exercised vigorously every day until the day he died; a beautiful young woman limited by spina bifida but determined to hit the weights; and a retired senior Marine officer who stands as a shining example of the best the armed forces has to offer and the kind of person we all strive to be. We've also come to know and admire a black university professor who is at the top of his profession; a retired World War II combat veteran and corporate executive who works out regularly despite several debilitating strokes and painful arthritis and keeps everyone laughing with his constant flow of quips and jokes; a buoyant woman whose ready smile and cheerfulness light up every room she enters; a gentle Lebanese man who taught us never to judge by appearances; a retired seventy-four-year-old biochemist whose personality, intellect, and powerful strength seem to be forever youthful; and many others. I know there will be many more such people to admire and emulate and more lessons to be learned because we have chosen to struggle and sweat together and to befriend each other in a great good gym.

THE GREAT GOOD GYM

DOING IT TOGETHER

When you come face-to-face with another's intense struggle for health, strength, and appeal, it reveals what kind of person you are. It's difficult to be indifferent to another's effort when you are also straining in the same effort. Knowing how difficult it is to get into shape, you feel empathy for other members. As you commiserate about the frustrations of exercising, the strains and injuries, and the effects of aging, you encourage each other to persevere and to triumph as much as you can. You admire others for subjecting themselves to the rigors of exercise because you have done those very same exercises, and you know exactly how they feel. You gain a particular respect for the older exercisers who persevere tenaciously well past their primes. You soon realize that you have many qualities, feelings, and experiences in common with the other members. These commonalties and your mutual efforts to improve by exercising help bring about mutual understanding and supportiveness, as well as compassion, ready humor, and friendliness.

Our great good gym is filled with good humor and good times intermingled with frequent grunts and groans. While grimaces from straining may outnumber the smiles, it is often a close race. Serving as quick relief from the strain of an exercise set, humor is ubiquitous in our gym. It distracts us from our bodies and renews our spirits.

Each exerciser competes against himself, his last performance, or his ultimate goals. Good-natured competition occurs among friends of approximate abilities. We compete with our friends so we will work harder to do our best and cheer others on with fervor and goodwill even in contests we are participating in. Our friends' successes, even when they top ours, push us to work harder in the future. It's a reciprocal relationship; we want the best from them and for them, and their best always brings out our best.

Any gym has the potential to become a great good gym, where everyone is welcome and can work to reach their highest physical and human potential. The great good gym attracts the best of people and brings out the best in people. Strenuous exercising deepens your character and enhances your personality. While the body is tested, exhausted, and strengthened by the workout, the spirit and psyche are elevated to a higher level, both during and after exercising at the great good gym. Filled with many friendly acquaintances who create a fun, warm, and happy atmosphere, the gym feels just like home to its members during the time they spend there.

While most people worry about being accepted by others, it is more important to learn how to bring out the best in others while sharing the best of yourself. The great good gym is a perfect place both to experience this and to practice it. The gym is unique in that offers abundant opportunities to show your best qualities and to receive the best from your sweaty fellow exercisers . . . as you grunt, groan, and grimace together.

Enjoying live music and camaraderie at the Neutral Ground.

The Neutral Ground Coffee House

NEW ORLEANS, LOUISIANA

ROBERT FROST was once asked by Edward R. Murrow to name the worst word in the English language. I'm sure the question was prearranged, but for effect, Frost pretended to make a major task of it before answering, "exclusive." Hating constructions that divide humanity, Frost would have loved the New Orleans Neutral Ground Coffee House. One will not find a more inclusive establishment than this and it has offered music and bonhomie for a quarter of a century now.

Unlike the other coffeehouses described in this collection, the Neutral Ground is a cooperative in which the membership assumes responsibility for its continued existence. Though it is usual for patrons of a third place to think of it as theirs, in this case it's literally true. Responsibility for keeping it going is often onerous and worrisome. Indeed, co-op manager Barbara Mattingly confesses that this third place often seems more like a daily struggle than a victory. But even the struggle can be a plus for, as the Kettering studies of community teach us, major problems, when collectively solved, give rise to the power and importance of "We," which is all too rare in our contemporary culture.

I remember my visit to the Neutral Ground some years ago at Ms. Mattingly's kind invitation. The place opened at 8:00 in the evening and some friends and I arrived shortly thereafter. No sooner had we settled in than the door opened and young parents appeared with small children who immediately darted off in glee to greet fictive "aunts" and "uncles." This was not a family reunion, I had to remind myself, but a third place in the best sense. I also recall that a young woman of extraordinary beauty got no more attention than anyone else; that some teenagers were cloistered in a large back corner booth like mafioso capos; and that the "Chicken Lady" was absolutely charming as she put her rubber pet through its paces for the newcomers. Ms. Mattingly does not identify the Chicken Lady here, but if you drop in some evening you're very likely to meet her.

EVOLUTION

Greta opened the Penny Post Coffee House in the winter of 1974–75 in an old New Orleans neighborhood that combined residential and small commercial use. The rented building had the advantage of having been a house and its many rooms favored a variety of activities including live music, card games, backgammon, chess, and chatting. The "'60s culture" took root in New Orleans during the '70s and the Penny Post resembled the typical bohemian coffeehouse. Pastries, coffees, teas, and other nonalcoholic beverages were on the menu.

The Penny Post attracted people from a broad area and many who lived within walking distance. Its regulars became like family. A kitchen fire in 1977 caused extensive damage and Greta decided to move on to other things. Realizing what she had created, Greta wisely and graciously offered the business to the devoted group of regulars with the suggestion that they operate it as a cooperative. As the fire damage was extensive, a new location was sought and found about two miles away. It was an unlikely area, even less commercial than the original and almost entirely residential. As before, many neighborhood residents became regular patrons who strolled over whenever they wanted a cup of coffee and the opportunity to chat with someone. Also, many of the regulars moved into the neighborhood to be close to the Penny Post.

The building at the new location had once housed a popular bar that was itself a third place for many students from two nearby universities. Eventually, however, problems developed with the neighbors and it was closed down. The owner then remodeled to accommodate two coffeehouses where there had been one tavern. He built a wall down the middle with half of the original oval bar serving one side, and the other half serving the other side. Both places attracted very faithful but very separate groups of customers. Our side continued as the Penny Post while the other offered a beatnik atmosphere featuring poetry readings and short plays. Like its earlier version, the Post opened nightly, featuring acoustic music, coffees, teas, and pastries, now home-baked by the co-op's volunteers.

A state charter called for an annually elected board whose monthly meetings were open to all members. The Post was open to the public and all were welcome to join the co-op. There was no cover charge and membership fees were kept low so that the Post would be a more inclusive third place. Members were encouraged to volunteer for a variety of jobs necessary to running the business and were rewarded with reduced food and beverage prices and receipt of a monthly newsletter featuring the music schedule. Most important, though, members were part of the "in" group, the "family," which at one time numbered as many as three hundred.

The major foci of the coffeehouse were coffee, camaraderie, and acoustic music. The music was mostly traditional folk and bluegrass and what we called "homemade music," now commonly described as "contemporary folk." For years, the Post was the only venue in New Orleans for local singer/songwriters of contemporary folk music. Weekly "open mic" nights were open to any musicians as an informal audition. Weekend sets were generally granted by invitation, but weeknights were liberally scheduled. We hosted some high-quality musicians, but often we didn't have enough to fill the calendar. We were open six nights a week, three musicians per night.

Many a night after closing time, a handful of regulars stayed, unwilling to end a stimulating rap session. As in the original Penny Post, jigsaw puzzles and games of chess, backgammon, and cards were provided. People felt free to bring their own games while others brought books or homework and sat in the quieter areas to read. Unfortunately, the new location did not have separate rooms, though some areas were partially walled off. The music and the conversation sometimes interfered with each other, perpetuating a running controversy: Which is more important, the conversation or the music? The question was never settled and I think we all came to realize that the Post wouldn't be the Post without both.

As in any volunteer organization, there were problems. A few people did most of the work and there were cliques and factions stemming from different opinions about how to run the business. Some wanted more structure and money, but others felt that would be almost immoral, that the co-op should be run on "good vibrations" and love of fellow man. The latter didn't want prices raised lest poorer patrons be discouraged from joining or attending.

Things would start to look bleak, the rent would be overdue and the board would have to call an emergency meeting. Then people would rally, new volunteers would come forth, and things would go smoothly for a while. But in 1992, the financial problems became very serious. Morale was low and few regulars were showing up. There was little doubt that, after fourteen years, this was the end of the Penny Post. It was a sad time for us all—but there were a few already at work. . . .

A group of the former Penny Post members wanted a coffeehouse with improved business practices while retaining the warm and casual ambiance of the Penny Post. Even as the Post was dying, phone calls were being made. Eventually, a meeting of about twenty former members was called and a new co-op was soon to be born. The landlord who had evicted the Penny Post was consulted, and after a two-month hiatus the spruced-up establishment reopened as the Neutral Ground Coffee House. There was one glitch. Notices of the opening had been mailed but the legal paperwork permitting sales was incomplete. Fred, the new president of the board of directors, suggested that we go ahead with the opening but, to keep things legal, not sell anything—just give it away opening night. There was a large turnout and the Neutral Ground was launched with a joyous *esprit de corps*.

Though much like the old co-op in many ways, the Neutral Ground enjoys improved business practices and a charter that provides for a paid manager. The manager's salary is low, but it ensures stability in this most important of jobs. The furnishings of the Neutral Ground remain, as before, a hodgepodge of donations, but it's a new and clean hodgepodge. Ceilings and counters were repaired, lighting was improved, and art shows now grace the long brick and cypress walls.

A stage was not added. We wished to keep the musicians separated from the audience by mere inches; that is, to keep them "connected." The music is still live and free but we're more discriminating now and consistently provide great listening. The acoustic guitar reigns supreme, but a greater variety of instruments now add their sounds. The first Friday of every month is Blues Nite and occasionally there is a "Wemin Making Music" night when all three sets are performed by female singer/songwriters. On one of those "wemin" nights, a gay male duo dressed in drag performed a humorous set. They were not only allowed, they were encouraged.

Among our original organizers is a man who teaches at a local medical school and whose avocation is bluegrass. He draws a changing troupe of musicians from the current crop of students and they make regular appearances at the Neutral Ground, attracting a large following and creating a festive evening. They bill as "Wabash" but the regulars refer to "Bagwellian Night" in honor of the good professor's name.

Higher music standards bring a greater number of quality musicians and attract more people to the coffeehouse. We are on an informal coffeehouse circuit where musicians travel state to state to play scheduled gigs at small venues. We are proud that some of our musicians have succeeded in the music world. Bill Malone was already recognized as the world's foremost authority on the history of U.S. country music when he played at the Penny Post while teaching at Tulane University. Lucinda Williams became a nationally recognized songwriter. Emily Saliers went on to win a Grammy Award and recorded numerous CDs as part of the popular duo the Indigo Girls. Some Neutral Ground musicians have won singer/songwriter contests around the country. Many have won first and second place local awards from *Off Beat*, an international music magazine. The Neutral Ground itself has won first place *Off Beat* awards for best music venue of its kind in New Orleans. We have produced our own *Live at the Neutral Ground* CD, consisting of fourteen artists' songs, twelve of which are originals. And now we have a Web site run by Julie, our barefoot webmistress.

THE SUSTAINING APPEAL

$\mathcal{I}t$ is the atmosphere, ambience, and the attitude of the Neutral Ground that has changed the least. Our goals are the same as in the original Penny Post—to provide a friendly place to gather, a home away from home, and a place for amateur as well as experienced songwriters and musicians to perform. That it is a friendly place may be judged by the amount of time it takes, upon arrival, to work your way to the counter and order coffee. There are many regulars to greet along the way, and departures are almost as lengthy for the same reason.

The name "Neutral Ground" is appropriate to our unchanging policy regarding membership. We are inclusive and nonjudgmental. Patrons respond to each other according to who, rather than what, they are. Age, race, socioeconomic status, career, mental health (or lack thereof), education, sexual orientation—none of this matters. "Neutral Ground" has double meaning in that street medians in New Orleans are known by the same name and they enjoy public use for strolling, jogging, dog walking, and, on one avenue, for gathering to catch the trolley that runs down the center. In our coffeehouse as on those medians, one finds a generous mix of humanity. At any of our tables you may find a lawyer, a carpenter, a high school counselor, or a clerical worker engaged in conversation.

Though geared for adults, the Neutral Ground is also suitable for families and their children. Our youngest regulars are two elementary schoolchildren who've known us all since they were preschoolers and who, even then, treated us as if we were peers. Leaving their parents the moment they enter the door, they circulate throughout the evening just like everyone else.

Just across the street live two preteen brothers who are always up for chess or card games. Though their mother seldom comes with them, she knows where they are at night. Eleanor, a newly divorced mother of five, became a regular at the Penny Post because she needed a place where she and her children could go together, and she even became our manager for a time. Twenty years later, she has moved away, but one of her daughters, now an adult, comes to the Neutral Ground as a vocalist in a very popular band.

I doubt if our third place atmosphere would have developed as well, if at all, if either of our locations had been in a contemporary commercial strip. For me, a visit to a mall or a shopping center is a business trip. I wish only to make my purchases and leave, and while there, I never expect to engage in interesting conversations, much less cultivate friendships. I think third places thrive best in a more leisurely atmosphere.

Certainly, the choice that many members make to move into housing close by the coffeehouse has been facilitated by our location. The desirability of having one's third place near one's home seems lost upon those who write and administer modern zoning ordinances.

The allure of the Neutral Ground is sustained, also, by the fact that it is a place apart, a world unto itself, with a culture of its own, often humorous, often poignant. Julie, a veteran member, recalls when the Penny Post had no telephone, a "lack" that she appreciated and which helped preserve our coffeehouse as a place apart. Paul has the same fond memory of that phoneless retreat.

Julie also recalls our days in the more bohemian atmosphere of the Penny Post and its Sunday sing-alongs. Vivid in her mind were all those people sitting sideways at the bar, each person giving the person in front a back rub. Then, after five or ten minutes, someone would shout "Turn" and they would swing around so that the line faced the opposite direction and nobody got left out.

New members know nothing of the "salad bar," "Gorilla George," "King James," or other features of earlier days until the coffeehouse lore is shared with them. The "salad bar" was a multiple urinal in the unisex bathroom, eventually replaced with a single unit. "Gorilla George" came to life one Halloween night when someone climbed upon the bar and put a gorilla mask over a tall floor lamp that stood on the bar. The mask was thin enough to glow and, of course, light poured out of the eye and mouth holes. Whether out of laziness or design, no one ever took it down and soon enough the first item written on the set-up instructions for the bar was "Turn on Gorilla George," thus ensuring a good night.

Time and the effects of the light bulb eventually caused George to deteriorate. He just dried right up. You'd be sitting at the end of the bar drinking coffee and a piece of George would fall into your cup. Finally, George had to be laid to rest. He now lies in an old Schwegmann's grocery bag in the back of Julie's closet but will never be forgotten.

A lot of characters come through our door, some transient and obnoxious, but once in a while, someone will walk through the door and into your heart. Enter King James. To the unknowing eye, James didn't have a whole lot going on. He was afflicted with a mental condition that left him gaunt and shaky. He'd sit off by himself for long periods, not speaking, just smoking incessantly and slurping his coffee. When he did speak, it was often something so far out that you weren't sure how to respond. But there were surprising depths to James. Julie says that he was probably the smartest person she's ever known. She played Trivial Pursuit with him once and vowed never to do it again. He missed one obscure question by only a few numbers. The more you talked to James, the more you realized that when he sat off in the corner, smoking and slurping, he wasn't just in his own little world. He was paying attention. He knew things, things you'd never expect him to remember. "How're your mom and dad? Linda and Bruce, right? Did your mom get over her cold?" He was always ready with a hug or a pat on the back and a big toothy grin.

King James exemplified the old saying, "Don't judge a book by its cover." If you do, you risk missing out on a treasure. James is gone now and very much missed. He was a bright star in our universe that may never have shone had it not been for our coffeehouse. After his death, relatives thanked us for including James and told us that he would not have lived nearly as long as he did but for the life our place offered.

Our oldest member was Mr. Arthur. "How ya doin' ta' night, Mista Awtha?" always evoked an air of worried concern, muttered in short, fast, choppy sentences. It was difficult to know what Mr. Arthur was talking about. He would sit at a table and mutter to anyone—or no one—sitting across from him. He walked like he talked: in short, quick bursts. No one knew anything about him except that he lived within walking distance. But he was one of our regulars off and on and everyone talked to him. It was sad when he had been absent for too long and we realized we'd not see him again. We were consoled in knowing that our coffeehouse had provided a safe place that he could walk to and be accepted, "socializing" in his own way. If not for our place, where would he have gone?

THE CHALLENGE OF TEENAGERS

Most third places don't cater to adolescents these days and that's a pity. On the other hand, teenagers are often the hardest age group to include, partly because they often choose to hang out by themselves, and partly because adults in American society don't relate to them very well.

To illustrate the potential that inclusive third places have for the social development of adolescents, let me turn the discussion over to Julie and let her explain in her own words:

> It's amazing how one little thing can change your whole life. For me that thing was the Penny Post Coffee House. When I was a junior in high school (during '77 or '78), I, along with a couple of friends, started taking guitar lessons from Kim, who played at the Penny Post. Kim decided that we were going to give our group a name and have a "recital" of sorts at the Post. So he signed us up and the next thing we knew, we were 2000 Proof, one teacher on lead vocals and guitar backed up by four extremely nervous high school girls strumming in unison and singing occasional backup harmonies. We played our first gig at the Penny Post with proud parents looking extremely out of place, eyeing the cushions, then deciding it best to snag bar stools instead. My friend Kathleen and I were so taken with the Post that we started going every chance we got, which was often. It became our third place (and we didn't even know what a third place was). We continued with the music, often filling in for no-show performers. We worked the counter, eventually served on the board, and, of course, we just hung out. If every teenager had a Penny Post this would be a much better world. Being a part of a cooperative consisting of such a wide variety of people and being involved in multiple aspects of that cooperative has been one of the best learning experiences I've ever had. I've learned to accept the feelings and beliefs of others whether or not I agree with them (not always an easy lesson) and maybe most importantly, I've learned that no matter how different people are, deep inside we all want the same thing: to be loved and accepted for who we are.
>
> If it weren't for the Penny Post I probably would have gotten bored with my guitar, and my music would have been lost. But I was fortunate enough to find this wonderful little haven offering acceptance and encouragement (both musically and spiritually). There were moments of connection that were nothing less than religious. I can remember John singing his traditional closing song, "The

Weight," and inviting me (along with half the people in the room) up to the stage area to sing harmonies, and then inviting (or more correctly, demanding) everybody left in the audience to sing along as well. Those were some magical moments, everyone in the room in perfect sync (if not quite perfect harmony) and of one mind. It was an incredible feeling that will stay with me forever. There were times when Kathleen and I were on stage singing and we'd connect with perfect sync and harmony. Conversations would die down, all eyes would turn toward the stage, somewhere in the audience a sprinkling of voices sang along, and at that very moment we were all of one being. Some people never even come close to that feeling. This coffeehouse has given me the gift of more than my share of those magical moments. I met Richard, Susan, Carl, and Kent at the Penny Post. We began singing together as A Cut Above and we had our own moments of oneness with the Penny Post crowd. Since then I have been a member of other musical groups. Between the bands, the song circles, the sing-alongs, and the impromptu jam sessions, I've lost count of the number of musicians I have met, played with, learned from, and sometimes even taught, through the coffeehouse. I think my muse must live there. On those occasions when I wander away for a time, she somehow manages to guide me back.

High school students like Julie need us just as we need them to be part of our family. They don't have the resources to run a co-op coffeehouse by themselves. But in substantial numbers, they can present problems. The recent wave we've received at the Neutral Ground has literally displaced many of our customers and loyal patrons, as they took every seat and loitered outside at the entrance. Not making purchases, not joining the co-op, not volunteering, not even paying attention to the music, they did nothing but take up space. They were only using the Neutral Ground as a place to meet away from parental supervision. They didn't understand that it was a co-operative and that they weren't guests. Many paying customers stayed away. It was no longer their place. Finances went red.

Some of the students did participate, working behind the counter, playing music, and getting to know the other patrons. Regulars included them in card games and one was elected to the board. There are fewer high school students now, but for long-term patrons the question, "Which regulars will be there?" has become "Will anybody I know be there?" It's expected that the coffeehouse will change with time, but even if it ceases to be our third place, it should be somebody's third place.

Over a twenty-five-year period the zeitgeist changes. Bohemian is no longer "in." Co-ops faded like black light posters and Day-Glo paint. Instead of face-to-face human encounters, we now favor human to machine interface. Maybe the more dehumanized our society becomes, the more it will recognize the importance of third places. In spite of recent problems, the Neutral Ground is now on the verge of a new and promising future. A few old members are coming back. I'm hopeful for a renewed spirit so that our coffeehouse will always be a first-rate third place.

The Sharpest Irony

THROUGH A dear friend at Penn State, I learned about Denis Wood, who had intimate knowledge of a wonderful bookstore in Raleigh, North Carolina. Under the shelter of the front of the store were bins of books left out overnight with a box for coins that was used to support public radio. The bins of books also put life on the street after-hours, thus making for a safer neighborhood.

When I further learned that Denis was something of a renaissance man, a Ph.D. scholar whose work can be seen in over a hundred publications spanning a variety of fields, I knew I had gained a first-rate contributor. Then I learned something else. Denis had done two years in a minimum security prison and its third place character had sustained him against the privations and indignities of convict life. As he was willing to tell that story, I resolved to find a bookstore elsewhere in favor of the rare opportunity his misfortune presented.

His account contrasts with the brutal image of prison life that television consistently portrays, but you will not get the impression that prison life is in any way desirable. In life on the outside, the third place serves its function for the individual and for society when integrated with the first and second places that are home and work, respectively. In prison, that stabilizing tripod doesn't exist. In prison, the third place experience is born of desperation and despair due to both the present situation and the prospect of returning to life on the outside as an "ex-con."

I began to think about prison as a third place when Chicago said to me—it was in front of his dorm, we were sitting on a bench in the sun—"It's not like this in the world. In the world I couldn't sit with you for hours and talk about anything and we both enjoy it." In the world, he said, he wasn't always joking around like he was in prison. In the world he had responsibilities. In the world he was always serious, always hustling, always watching his back. I wouldn't even recognize him. I certainly wouldn't like him.

It was a theme to which he returned often, a theme echoed by many others: *the world was hard.* On the one hand were the streets, where so many of the young blacks I knew made their living. On the other hand was home, too often a site of parental censure, or of spousal claim.

Again and again I listened to stories of the streets getting hotter and hotter, of life at home getting harder and harder to take until . . . what? This one took a risk he knew was stupid, or that one grew less and less patient; and so this one got picked up at a Greyhound station, and that one got arrested at the mall; and so this one was sentenced to six to eight months for possession, and that one to ten to twelve months for assault. No one wants to be in prison, but you can sure "chill the fuck out while you there."

At the time I hadn't read Ray Oldenburg's *The Great Good Place,* but as a professor on a landscape architecture faculty, as an environmental psychologist, as a *lover of cities,* I'd toyed with not dissimilar ideas. Certainly I'd read reviews of *The Great Good Place,* and long pieces about it in magazines. I knew the term—*third place*—and that morning, listening to Chicago, the term came to mind. Prison was Chicago's third place. Other potential third places in his world—the clubs, the liquor houses, the mall—were each an extension of the street. To the extent that the street entered prison—and in North Carolina it wasn't much—it was muted. In prison Chicago didn't have to watch his back, and as long as he was there his women could send *him* money. It was cool. And so he could chill with me in the morning sun, talking, pointlessly (but with great élan) about nothing.

Not that we had nothing to do—we both had jobs—but it was Saturday and this is what we did, this is what everybody did, sat around and talked, and shot a little ball, and watched a little TV, and played a little cards, and laughed a lot. Whatever else we were doing we always laughed a lot. Maybe it was all the blacks, and laughter was a piece of the armor Cornel West writes about blacks wearing to beat back the demons of hopelessness, meaninglessness, and lovelessness, but I was so primed to laugh or make someone else laugh I had a smile playing on my lips the whole time I was there. It just made you feel light.

And thinking about this I began to see that prison wasn't just a third place for drug dealers to escape the duress of the street and the odium in which their families held them, it was a third place for all of us who live there.

It's curious. People think they know what prison's like. They imagine they must know what it's like. But when they try to say how it is that prisoners pass their day, all they come up with are platitudes. During the second of the twenty-five months I would end up serving, one of my more sophisticated acquaintances wrote to inquire about my . . . *contact with other human beings*. "Contact with other human beings?" I shot back, "I've never had so much contact with other human beings in my life! I've been three weeks in jail and four here at Troy, and in both places I've lived with thirty or forty other guys in complete intimacy. Here at Troy I'm also in lesser contact with the larger population with which I mingle on the ball field, in the yard, the gym, the dining hall, the library, and other common spaces. And then there're the COs (that is, Correctional Officers)."

Part of the problem with our image of prison is that it's unitary: prison is like. . . . *this*. But it's not. Prison is a bunch of prisons, they're all different, and before prison there's jail. Because all kinds of criminals are locked up in jail, jails are maximum security places. Older jails are like the ones in the movies, barred cells in a row; but in newer jails the prisoners' rooms line the walls of two-tiered blocks (or pods as they're increasingly called), where, the common spaces convicts and detainees eat, watch TV, and play cards together. Most of the time there are four pods to a floor, but jails have as many floors as local sheriffs can cajole taxpayers into paying for. No matter how big they are, jails are never big enough.

The first prison after jail is more or less secure. It depends on the crime. I'm a felon (I had a sexual relationship with a teenage boy), so the prison to which I was sent for "processing" (the Troy mentioned above) was much like the jail in which I waited for the state to take me to prison, only the prison was older and less intelligently designed. Troy was what North Carolina calls "close custody," looser than maximum but tighter than medium. What happens in processing—among other things—is that you get "classified." They pegged me for minimum and in time I was shipped to a minimum custody camp. Minimum is the security level at which most juveniles and all misdemeanants process.

In all minimum and in most medium custody camps—to which I'd later be "busted back" for breaking rules—prisoners live in dormitories, that is, in big rooms filled with bunk beds. These dorms look exactly like old-fashioned military barracks or the cabins at summer camp. At least they do in North Carolina. It doesn't seem to be much different anywhere in the world.

So, in any prison term, you're going to spend at least some time in jail, some time in a processing center, and some time in a field camp, most likely in a number of field camps, for prisoners are in perpetual motion. You get promoted for good behavior, or demoted for bad, and they ship you from one camp to another. Or that camp offers you an opportunity this one doesn't so you put in for a transfer. Or there's another camp that's closer to home so you put in for a transfer. Or you just get tired of the camp you're at and you put in for a transfer. Some camps are okay and some aren't.

North Carolina, with a little over 30,000 inmates, maintains a scheduled bus system for moving prisoners around. Only a very small number of prisoners are confined to the great, old maximum security prisons; and ultimately—except for an even smaller number of death-row inmates, intractable psychotics, and thorough screw-ups—even guys with multiple-life sentences end up, after an odyssey through the archipelago of prison camps stretching across the state, in minimum security custody.

There's incessant motion within the camps too, even in jail. In jail the movement may be in chains, and in the more secure prisons if not in chains, then at scheduled times, but there are nonetheless trips to the yard, ball field, dining hall, library, gym, clothes house, canteen, visitation hall, church, nurse's station; and in many medium and all minimum security camps—where all these places can be accessed pretty much at will—outside jobs, in street clothes for those on work-release. The fact is, prison's little like people want to imagine, and if it's not quite like life on the street, it *is* like life in a third place, it's like living in a third place twenty-four hours a day, seven days a week. I mean, where else in America these days can you stroll out your front door on a fine spring evening and find the sidewalks pleasantly crowded with people almost all of whom know your name and greet you as you pass?

There aren't even *sidewalks* in that many places anymore.

"What's up, Professor?" guys cry and I can stop and chat or just and pass on by.

The air is full of laughter, but that knot over there is debating a fine point of Biblical exegesis and over there they're trying out a rap one of them has rhymed and that couple are lovers. There are no cars threatening the peace, no bass machine is rattling the windows, no one has a handgun stuck down the inside of his pants or on a shelf of the closet in his bedroom. The basketball court is thronged and down on the ball field two dorms are playing each other. There are guys on the weight pile and there is the clink of horseshoes.

If you could stroll down the hill with me from K-and-L, which is what my dorm at this camp was called, you would never imagine you were in prison. A military base you might guess, except that there are no ranks, everything is so casual, so comfortable. What is most impressive, most satisfying, is the open friendliness, the warmth. The small-town virtues whose loss is so bemoaned are alive and well here where competition is as low as it gets in America, and where naked mutual aid is more in evidence than anywhere except in the wake of a natural disaster. Only here it's all the time.

How many of the characteristics Oldenburg identifies as affording an engaging public life do prisons have? All of them, really. The interstitial spaces in prisons are filled with people sitting, standing, walking. None of the spaces in prison are reserved for that well-dressed middle-class crowd welcomed at today's shopping malls. Among those looking and doing well are the elderly, the poor, and the infirm, many of whom are granted sometimes extravagant signs of respect. It is, needless to say, a pedestrian environment. Tables with benches, benches, sitting-walls, stairs, railings, fences, and other places to sit or lean against are abundant at even the camps with the fewest amenities.

Moreover, prisons *abundantly exhibit* the features Oldenburg identifies as common and essential to third places: prison is emphatically neutral ground; it is the leveler par excellence; the main activity, almost of necessity, is conversation; it's accommodating (if not really accessible to the non-convict); the crowd is a regular one in several senses of "regular"; the profile is about as low as it gets; and the mood is playful almost to a fault (it's not easy to raise consciousness in prison). By law it's a home away from home.

I said that prison is *emphatically* neutral ground. It was one of the great things about prison. You could sit down anywhere and whatever one thought about your sitting down, it was cool. In Oldenburg's phrase, everyone was "fair game." It wasn't like on the street where sitting down at a stranger's table at a restaurant is. . . . *not done.* As the guys put it, *everything* in prison is the state's. If there was someone you'd seen in the yard that you wanted to know better and there was a seat at his table, or someone you'd never seen before, even in the dining hall, you could sit down and strike up a conversation.

There were dumb customs—"white on the right" was one of them—but whatever power they might have had, they didn't have anymore. That was in '96, '97 and '98. Sure, blacks tended to eat in one part of the hall and whites in another, but—and I'm white—I always ate on the black side except when I was eating with blacks who liked to eat on the white side. It was no big deal. It was just noisier and friendlier with the blacks. There were those who'd try to scare you away with their crazy eyes, and a few serious five-percenter types who'd get up and move if you sat down at their table, but that only happened twice, and who knows what their problem really was. They might have been offended by my crime and afraid observers would draw unwarranted conclusions about our relationship, or they might have been offended by my outspoken atheism, or my race, or my college education. They might have just wanted to be alone. But then, that's important too, since it's an important requirement of any good community that no one *has* to be part of it, especially not all the time.

Similarly, you never had to move. My first time on a road squad bus I sat in someone else's usual seat. I wasn't trying to start anything but I didn't know and anyhow . . . *how was this his seat?* I would soon come to appreciate the role of custom on these tiny, cramped buses—especially for these very big guys—but so strong was the superordinate principle that everything in prison is the state's that a resolution had to be *negotiated*: "Look, Professor, let the man have his seat. You come over here, sit by me."

On another occasion I did refuse to move when a guy I'd never seen before insisted on rolling out his prayer rug where I was reading on the grass. It got tense there for a second with him leaning over me with his fist cocked and my finger gone to mark my place in my book, but he thought better of it. After he'd said his prayers—a few feet away—he came over to apologize. He embraced me and said, "What I was thinking? I said my prayers here yesterday is all. It not like it's mine."

This type of attitude worked as a leveler. Although I'd been warned not to let people know what I was in for, in encouraging me to come clean my first night in jail, Chicago had said, "Cuz, we *all* in here for something." It was to be my experience that in prison one was valued for what he was. . . . *in prison* . . . not for what he'd done or what he'd been on the street. Other ideas, which some managed to retain through jail, vanished during processing. That's when the prison sent home the clothes you'd worn to jail, and your worldly status claims along with them. The longer one was in prison the less likely he was to assert, or be hobbled by, street wealth or position. What did poverty matter, what did education count for in the block where sociability, the ability to tell a story and a sense of humor were the essential, were the *only* currency?

Just as we were all in for something, it was taken for granted that we all had problems. We were expected to bear these without burdening others with them, and anyhow there was always someone, usually no more than a bunk away, whose difficulties made yours look like assets. At the same time this meant that *serious* pain was succored. At my lowest, gnawed by the unraveling of my life out in that world, I was lying on my bunk not even reading, just staring at the ceiling. That's when Jody brought me a cup of coffee: "We just want you to know we all love you, Professor."

Still, the sound you most heard inside was laughter; and if much of the humor was physical, a huge part of it was verbal, not jokes either, but rich humane situational humor—Richard Pryor humor—directed as much at ourselves as at each other. Is it that prisoners are self-selected storytellers? Or is it that by exercising this ability as they do in prison they just get good at it? Either way, there is no end to the storytelling in prison. Some, especially those who excelled at dramatizing the most inconsequential incident, may have stuck to their version of the truth; but others were fabulous inventors, creating for themselves life histories of luxuriant novelty. So frequently did Chicago certify his rich Rabelaisian fantasies with an emphatic: "This the truth, Professor!" that to tell me something true he'd have to say, "Professor, I need to tell you a lie."

Many of the meager spirits who support our prison system imagine it a serious threat to talk about removing the TVs from prison dayrooms. I can't support this as much as I hate television (the constant exposure was the hardest part of prison for me), because it would be felt as no more than another slap across the face of guys slapped across the face too many times already, but I don't really believe removing the TVs would make much difference. Prisoners are masters at entertaining themselves, because you learn how to have fun in prison or you go crazy; and since even when the guys are watching television what they're doing mostly is talking, the absence of TVs would really be no more than a boon for conversation. In fact, the change in prison life that made the biggest difference while I was there was the adoption of "silent" televisions you could hear only through headphones of appropriately tuned transistor radios. Without the blaring television and the need to talk above it, the dayrooms became much more attractive places. The social life improved.

Nor was the talk always, or even usually, casual. Storytelling was a constant, but so was debate. My fellows discussed, argued about, fought over everything. No topic was too private, no theme too recondite. Debaters made continuous appeal to their audience for verification. For me it was the ultimate leveler, since I had once been a well paid professor who made his living telling stories and debating points, and now any point I might be trying to make counted for nothing. In an argument about evolution I couldn't simply assert radiocarbon dates as I'd been used to in the classroom. I had to justify them, had to explain how they worked, until, deep into the decay properties of radioactive elements I'd be brought up with "What's this have to do with coming from monkeys? Answer me that, Professor, what's this have to do with us coming from monkeys?" While the guys might have allowed me to settle one of their arguments about, maybe, the number of states in the Union, when it came to evolution, education, religion, child development, sex, race, venereal disease, politics, justice, gender, *ad infinitum*, I had precisely the authority they had: only what I could get a witness to. The rest had been sent home with my street clothes.

Talk enveloped, talk invaded everything. Baseball games, horseshoes, basketball games, spades, tonk, weight lifting, each was a ground for the display of wit, of humor, of sarcasm, of insults, of oaths, of dramatic reenactments. A basket wasn't just two points. It provided the grounds for another—verbal—dunk. A Boston wasn't just a skunk. It made an occasion for a breathless exhibition of card-playing enthusiasm—an all-but religious enthusiasm—the cards slapped on the table and then the hand played all over again, orally, card by card. There were guys who could rehearse hands they'd played weeks, months, *years* ago.

Nor was this oral game played only on the basketball court or out in front of the dorm or in the dayroom. It was as often played on the next bunk, or two bunks over, or on a bunk across the aisle. It used to drive me nuts, especially if I'd been trying to read, but in the end it proved to be another pleasure that came with living in the dorm, the conversations I could listen to lying on my back, or join in by turning on my side. When I was thinking I was going to go crazy if Andy Parham wasn't released soon—it didn't matter where in the dorm he was, you were in his conversation—KO moved in. The thing was, though, these guys were genuinely funny, they roped you in no matter how irritated they made you, and there was time enough to return to your book when they went to shower, at which time you almost always realized your book was less interesting than you'd thought.

God, was there talk! It was always going on, on the bunk beneath you, at the CO's desk, in the dayroom, out in front of the dorm, all over the walks and stairs, down around the canteen, in the dining hall. There was always an incident to spark a verbal exchange, a game (or a remembered game) of cards, a misstep, a song heard the night before on the radio, the day's menu, a story from the newspaper, a new haircut. We talked about the forms of talk itself, the way someone said a word, or a phrase he used, someone's accent, or "the way he breathe man, you ever notice that?" "And the way he crack his neck?" We talked about it all, chewed it over, rehearsed it, hashed it out, laughed at it, or with it, or about it, in the line for breakfast, and out at the gate waiting to go to work, and during count when we were all on our bunks, and in the shower washing and laughing and splashing each other.

At night when everyone except you was asleep there was always the CO at his desk. He was happy to have someone to help him keep awake.

Some guys took longer to achieve this easy familiarity than others, but at one time or another every member of even the inner circle had been a new face in the dorm. It's prison courtesy to let a new man slip into dorm life in his own good time, but at the same time it's a very small world. I wasn't inside long—not compared to many—but by the time I left jail I was already to some degree a known commodity wherever I went. Moving into the dorm on the medium custody camp to which I'd been demoted thanks to my "shy bladder" (that is, my inability to produce a urine sample on demand), not only was I greeted at the door by Wave, an old friend from processing; not only was I assigned a bunk across from Ricardo, a guy I'd heard of who's shipped from my pod in jail not long before I got there (and with whom I was arguing about power and love even before I'd had a chance to put my bags down); but I was moving into a dorm Chicago had vacated only a couple of months before: everyone knew about the crazy professor. Returning nine months later to the minimum custody camp from which I'd been demoted, I was greeted like a prodigal son. I was reassigned to my old dorm. In addition to most of the guys who'd been there when I left I soon found—it's a small world—the best friend I'd made at the medium custody camp I was coming from. Nor as a sort of marginal, older, white intellectual could I have been considered a part of the young, black, hip-hop community dominating the prisons I was in. Yet from my very first hours in jail I was made to feel like a regular member of precisely this crowd.

I'm pretty sure this would not have been the case in the world, at a club, say where hanging with a geeky, white dweeb would have conferred less than zero social status, but less than zero status is what we all had in common in prison. Prison is about as far from "in" as places get. In minimum custody, guys with community visit passes or on work release dressed for the street. They put on outfits, Polo from socks to shirt, or Tommy Hilfiger, or Fubu, killer shoes (those would have been Nikes when I started my sentence, but by the time I left they were Tims, you know, *boots*, Timberlands), and the guys wore jewelry that didn't stop. Back on the camp all this finery went into the locker and back out came the prison greens. As they closed the door on their street clothes the guys also closed it on the face they'd put on to face the world and . . . *what a relief!*

As much as we all yearned for the street, there could be little unwinding there. It was always a show, one was always on display, and as a convict more on display than ever before. To the extent that camp was a third place, guys were glad to get back to it, to get back *to the dorm*, to get out of the costume, to take off the mask, to walk around in their boxers scratching themselves and joking with the others. Inside we were *all* convicts, there was less point to the display, and so there was less of it, none at all at night when, our guard finally down, we slept, some of us with our hands between our legs, others with our arms around a pillow, or all akimbo, limbs in every attitude, farting, moaning, muttering, twisting, turning over.

Even visits could be horrible, could deteriorate into an interminable pushing of increasingly incommensurable words back and forth across a table, home intruding too deeply for comfort, recrimination sensed even when left unspoken. Then, afterward, the mood could turn fey. Then that feeling that Dutch historian Johan Huizinga identified as being "apart together" in an exceptional situation, of sharing something important, or mutually withdrawing from the rest of the world and rejecting the usual norms, would be unusually strong. Then one felt what could never be said: that these worthless jerks were the finest guys you'd ever know, and this stinking dayroom the best place in the fucking world.

This is the ugly truth about prison, the truth that no one wants to admit, that while being yanked out of your life is terrible, it's really okay inside, it's a third place in a world with too few third places, a world with too much work, a world with too many aspirations, and no way to be yourself. Only an idiot would ascribe the numbers we've got locked up to the dearth of third places in this country, but only a fool would refuse to see the connection. Only a fool would refuse to acknowledge that in a society in which men are treated like tools, men might find in the world of the prison dayroom a more decent place, one more accepting of people for their own sake, a place where hour for hour they could have more fun than anywhere else.

"Why when we in the world we can't have good, clean fun like this?" Gator asked. We'd come out to the ball field where his unit was playing mine. It was a gorgeous day. As we topped the rise the sky opened out before us, vast and hard blue and chockablock with nimbostratus going nuts with the sun, morphing, rays flashing, edges turning brilliant silver. From way back at the plate came a CRACK! as Hawk knocked one high in the sky and all the white-shirted players moved on the field of green. I hadn't known what to tell Gator then, but the simple fact is *there's no place in the world* for it, and I don't mean no ball field. I mean that the spatial order of modern life makes it impossible for men to wander out of their houses and find themselves spontaneously playing ball the way it's possible in prison, to find themselves playing ball, or spontaneously doing anything at all.

It's all about money in the world, and it's hard to make money out of guys playing ball, or singing together around a bench, or playing cards around a table, or leaning against a wall talking. It's hard to make money unless you can get them into a car, sell them a little gasoline, make them drive a little to do anything at all. There's little money to be made from the spontaneous social life of people.

To observe that this life is abundant in prison is not to praise prison. It is no more than to mourn the reality that only in prisons is there much of a remnant of the spatial order of face-to-face society, of the small town, of the lived-in neighborhood. Stripped of work and home, this order is that of the third place, and if once upon a time this public place was *the* place, at no time did this place exist without its complements of work and home. That prison has managed to retain the character of a third place *may* go a long way to explaining why prisoners do not tear their prisons down, but this does thereby not make a prison supportable. "What sane man," George Bernard Shaw asked, "would accept an offer of free board, lodging, clothing, waiters in abundance at the touch of a bell . . . even at the very best of Ritz Hotels, if the condition were that he should never leave the hotel?"

The cruelty of imprisonment—which those who have not experienced it cannot imagine—comes not from material deprivation or physical hardship but from the loss of the first and second places. The compensations of the third place are a balm but not panacea, and in the end they cannot make up for the loss of work and home in the context of which alone, after all, third places make their truest meanings.

Only in the modern world has the third place, as an assured part of daily life, been locked away from those who need it most, and granted fully only to those incapable of experiencing the first and second places. Among the ironies of our time, this has to rank among the sharpest.

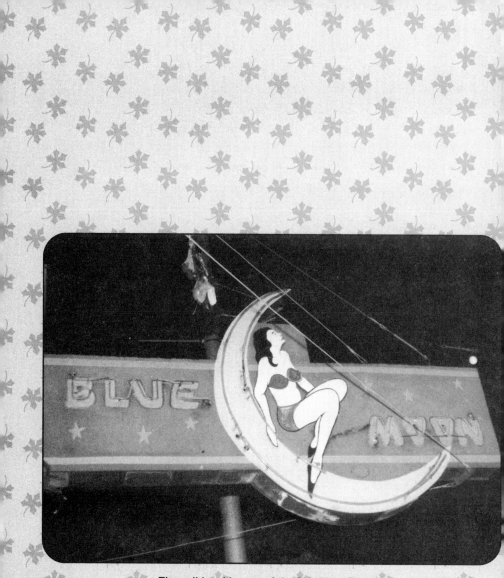

The well-loved beacon of the Blue Moon Tavern.

The Blue Moon Tavern

SEATTLE, WASHINGTON

IN THE late winter of 1990, I was invited to Seattle by the Forever Blue Moon Committee to help rescue "The Moon" from imminent destruction, and thanks to the efforts coordinated by Walt Crowley, the committee was successful. When I arrived in town, I was immediately transported to the tavern. Only its spaciousness obscured its resemblance to the crude warming shack abutting the skating rink in the hometown of my youth. Also different was the fact that the roof didn't leak in our warming shack. It was not immediately obvious why The Blue Moon should be spared.

As I looked more closely, however, I saw indications that this place was not exactly the dive local puritans took it to be. At a table near the front door sat a full-blooded Indian and the chairman of the political science department at the University of Washington absorbed in a game of chess. On the walls here and there was graffiti in Greek that, I was informed, many customers read without difficulty. Also on the surrounding walls were books that customers were free to borrow. On the right rear wall above the booths was the original Blue Moon sign, long since too large to satisfy the local code but too important an icon to be trashed.

I also took note of some bullet holes in the metal lampshade above the first of the two pool tables. With some experience in such matters, I judged them to have been made by a .38 special or 9mm weapon. Hmmm!

The room was chilly and when I suggested turning up the heat, I discovered there wasn't any. Management counted on human bodies to warm the place and indeed they did. It wasn't long before a multitude of human heaters appeared for another evening at The Moon.

The nightly invasion of The Moon takes place early in the evening and evolves into something of a social and conversational wonderland. Blue-collar mix with professional, women circulate freely with nobody hitting on them; every booth is animated and several regulars make the rounds with long stops at each booth. I was told that The Moon provides just two things, beer and conversation, and that a previous owner drove the regulars away by introducing food. On a subsequent visit, I noted that wine had snuck its way in and seemed to be gaining ground, but the staple is, and will remain, beers with taste to them.

The Blue Moon is thus an anomaly contradicting current wisdom about tavern operations. The Moon does not offer food. It has none of the ambience of those pretty pubs that lead the way in the upscaling of American bars. It does not advertise. It does not rely upon a variety of draws to entice new customers. What it does have, however, is a management that maintains the place as a Preserve for the First Rate Conversation in a society where most of the talk one hears is rather pitiful. That, I think, is its secret.

The bullet holes in the lamp shade? Nothing to be alarmed about. Some years ago a rat was spotted on the premises and so one of the owners and a few friends waited up after closing with a revolver at hand. Time passed and the rat didn't show. More time passed and still no rat and . . . well, one just can't allow boredom to creep into The Moon.

To approach the Blue Moon Tavern at night is to see a sagging brick building lit by a disarray of garish neon beer signs. Inside it doesn't get any better, by day or night. Concrete floors, booths casually assembled out of two-by-tens and whittled to near indecipherability by generations of carvers, a brass-railed bar that looks like it came from the set of a spaghetti western after the shoot-out, walls of cartoon and comic genius and a ceiling covered with old posters and everything stained by cigarette smoke into an obscurity usually reserved for ex-congressmen make this place objectively a "dive." Yet, most patrons call it their living room. The Moon doesn't brag about itself and has as its only boast that it features "live conversation." It may not look like much, but it sure does a lot of talking.

Although it is located close to the University of Washington's main campus in Seattle, underclassmen are not a large part of the Moon's clientele. Professors, graduate students, and research scientists are the more likely to sit elbow to elbow at the bar with the construction trades people, striking steelworkers, unreformed bookstore owners, literate marines, fishermen, and the usual bunch of poets (ASL and speaking), musicians, and artists, some of whom can almost afford the beer. You are as likely to hear a retired gas company repairman talk about singing folk songs in a yurt in Mongolia as a carpenter explaining to a drywaller in pretty convincing detail the coming collapse of technology stocks. The lady who works in the hair salon will be kicking butt on the pool table, someone will be practicing guitar in a back booth, cheers will erupt over a televised ball game, the guy who practices violin but doesn't speak English has come in because he feels comfortable here, a conversation in German can be going on at one side of the bar while one in Spanish is going on at the other, an intense political debate requiring great quantities of tobacco and pitchers of swill du jour rages on in a side booth, members of a club may be in the Blue Room laughing over outrageous jokes, beneath the painting of Theodore Roethke a couple of bikers discuss salvation for their woefully soulful Harleys while waiting to get on to the pool table, and a lawyer might denounce the incredible narrow-mindedness of a judge and the inscrutable behavior of juries to a lady who sells flowers to DINKs. Live conversation, however you pronounce it.

A few years back, a travel writer for the London Observer described the Blue Moon as "scabrous" and more authentically Soho than the pubs where the famous hang out in Soho. Implied in this observation is an element of what constitutes a third place and what makes a tavern like the Blue Moon interesting. If the fame of its clientele were an ingredient in making a great good place, the Moon would qualify on that alone. Photographs of the Pulitzer Prize–winning poets and other assorted writers who drank there in the past cover the valance over the bar. Undoubtedly there will be more. The story has been told more than once about the poet Theodore Roethke, who, upon being informed of winning Yale University's Bollingen Prize, announced to his class, "I have just won the Bollingen. To the Moon to celebrate." And indeed they did. Yet these greats and near greats are less likely to come up in conversation than the import of eigenvectors in statistics. Certainly they are talked about, but not as the only focus of conversation. Famous people can only have so much effect on an establishment. Ultimately all customers define the place they are in, as it ineluctably begins to redefine them. They bring in pictures or other memorabilia to hang on the wall, perhaps carve the initials of some half-remembered object of romantic adoration on a booth, or in some cases, carve a fair likeness. There are layers of these items concealing each other like the leaves of an artichoke being uneaten in a film running backwards.

At "Dirty Dick's and Sloppy Joe's," where they used to "drink their liquor straight," it wasn't funkiness or decrepitude that made it a place to hang out in, either. "Some went home with Marjorie, and, alas, some went home with Kate." It is the "alas" that makes that line, and it is an "alas" that is sighed by the place you're in, as well as the pose of your expectant lips.

Strangers stroll in, and a few hours later they march home two by two. Like a song played over and over again on an old jukebox, the ambience of a place soon fades from consciousness and the intoxicating burr of intermingled conversation fills the ears. As the poet David Wagoner noted in explaining the Blue Moon's ambient din and its effects, "It was so noisy it might as well have been quiet."

The emotional memories that are the glue of language are in an end-less feedback loop with our surroundings. Some people need the rein-forcement of traditional families, some the challenge of their careers, some the comfort of their watering hole, and for some a combination. From its beginning in post-Prohibition Seattle, the Blue Moon has appealed to those appalled by the men in gray flannel suits. With local prizefighters overseeing them, the rowdies of the thirties made the Blue Moon the second most popular (by volume) tavern in town. The forties saw the Moon filled with soldiers and sailors (it was an integrated bar even back then) during World War II who became the beatniks of the fifties and sixties who segued into the counterculture of the seventies. Now fragments of all these groups mingle to converse and perhaps plan the next great moment to cast into upheaval a time that needs more than greed to define itself.

The Blue Moon, like other traditional gathering places, is a well-polished button on the breast of its neighborhood. Whatever its original design it has been buffed to a degree that allows most folks to slide into it and become part of its fascination. A fellow raised in Portland, Oregon, but now living in Vancouver, British Columbia, always stops in when making his intercity transit. "I've got to recharge my batteries," he says, and slides into a booth, introducing a new friend to old ones and dissolving into the worn benches and warm conversation. An old-timer reminisces about seeing on a bathroom wall in Spain someone's lament, "I can't stand any more of this. I'm going home to the Blue Moon in Seattle." After all, as the graffito in the men's john once said, "Some nights the Moon howls, and the wolves are silent."

No establishment worthy of being a great good place is about any one individual. The firmament that is a third place is the accumulation of stars, the reflected glory of the sun, and the occasional brilliant flash of a comet or meteor. The Blue Moon has had more than its fair share of scintillating lights: a constellation of Pulitzer Prize winners in Theodore Roethke, Stanley Kunitz, Gary Snyder, and Carolyn Kizer. In the past few years one could have shared a beer and conversation with Calvin Trillin, Tom Robbins, or William Least Heat Moon. But no matter how many first-order magnitude stars populate the night sky, it is the myriad unnamed others that give it its shimmering essence.

In 1934 with the bells of Prohibition's repeal still reverberating, twenty-one-year-old Henry J. Reverman and partner Monty Fairchild opened the Blue Moon Tavern. Hank Reverman had taken three thousand dollars his father had set aside for a college education and started a tavern instead. "From the first day I opened the place it was filled with poets, and oddballs, and such like," he observed years later. Reverman continued by observing that no matter what he and his partner had imagined their clientele would be like, it didn't turn out that way. Whether it was the name, or the location one mile from the center of the University of Washington campus on a major east/west thoroughfare, or unknown forces, the Blue Moon has been catering to those sort of folks ever since.

Hank is far too modest to admit that perhaps his own warm and open personality had anything to do with the tavern's success. His is the kind of congeniality that makes people who don't know anyone in the place feel comfortable and start talking. As often as not, when a stranger walks into a neighborhood tavern for the first time, conversations are put on hold, the jukebox stops, heads turn, and the bartender becomes preoccupied removing an invisible speck from a glittering glass. The silence could peel the paint off of an old metal beer sign, and the trepidation could make someone wish for the first time in their lives that they were actually a salesman. However, the Blue Moon isn't like this. From Reverman's glory days to today the tavern has always had enough room for at least one more person to belly up to the bar and join the talk. At least theoretically they can do this, since in practical truth the bar is often three or four people deep, and it can be a strategic challenge to access and get the bartender's attention.

Fortunately, the staff is attentive and can spot the beerless through a maze of undulating conversant people. The success of the Blue Moon was only a start for Reverman. After dabbling in a few other taverns he took flying lessons and became an accomplished pilot. The advent of World War II put Reverman's newly acquired skills to good use. He enlisted in the Army Air Corps and became a flight instructor helping to prepare his nation for its greatest struggle. After the war he started Lake Union Flying Service operating charter flights and ferrying people to the waterfront cities and remote lakes of the Pacific Northwest. Now in his late eighties, he is still vital and active and maintains his own plane for a few annual flights. He still drops by the Blue Moon and has a schooner of beer on occasion and tells the tales of his interesting life.

People come and go and recluster in different arrangements: They wade up to the bar, chat with two or three acquaintances, get a pitcher, and join other friends in a booth elsewhere in the tavern. The next pitcher finds them talking to others while waiting for their beer, and at yet another booth to drink it. A booth crowded with geneticists might be discussing in the minutest detail the fold of a particular protein. A truck driver explains to a carpenter the relationship of Egyptian hieroglyphs to demotic script. A sports broadcast on television is being debated and cheered by others. It seems as if almost anything is possible.

World War II saw the Blue Moon become the "den mother" to a whole new set of troops. The shipyards and aircraft factories were busy and on the east side of the university campus along Lake Washington the Sand Point Naval Air station was in full swing. A wall-length mural, painted by a couple of sailors for seven pitchers of beer, still testifies to the Blue

Moon's place in helping to calm the edginess of the service personnel in a difficult time.

When McCarthyism swept the nation, its powerful undertow launched a wave of emotion in Washington State as well. As the GI Bill swelled the ranks of colleges with some fairly unlikely underclassmen and professors, the Canwell Committee began its limitless search for Bolsheviks and anything with even the slightest hint of red in it. That the decline of the pink salmon run cannot be traced directly back to Canwell is a surprise. Among other things this added an intense layer of politics to the various strata of the Blue Moon, as it found itself becoming a haven for the collateral damage left by the efforts of the humorless and indefatigable right-wing politicians.

Joe Butterworth was a Chaucerian scholar and member of the University of Washington department of English. It is difficult to assess from this remove what part of the Parliament of Fowls may have offended the Canwell Committee and moved them to blacklist Butterworth, but they did and he lost his job. He did not, however, lose his sense of humor nor his thirst for beer and companionship. His firing moved him a mile west, where he settled in at the Blue Moon's bar and used it as his writing desk. The Middle English of Chaucer wouldn't do, so he went for Old English and translated Marx's Communist Manifesto into Anglo-Saxon. As he was doing this, other patrons were watching the Army/McCarthy hearings on the tavern's television as if it were a sporting event. Occasionally cheers would erupt as Joseph Welch scored against Senator McCarthy.

The Bohemians who inhabited the Blue Moon in the fifties slowly gave way to a new generation of nonconformists. The 1960s saw the advent of "fringies," hippies, student activists who had been energized by the Civil Rights movement, and a variety of other radicals. The generation gap that so befuddled parents in this era was playing out on the pool tables and in the booths of the Blue Moon in a haze of smoke, a clank of glassware, and a froth of slogans and songs. One durable survivor of the Canwell Committee hearings, and found at the center of much of this turmoil and joy, was Stan Iverson. The bastard son of a socialist Montana sheriff, Iverson was a living reminder of the brutality that had been visited upon the working people of the Mountain West by timber, cattle, and mining interests. He was always happy to break into a Wobbly (World War I) song even if he couldn't carry a note in his rucksack. Time spent with the Communist Party led him ineluctably, although circuitously, to anarchist sensibilities. He would regale young radicals with his tales of old Socialist campaigns, police beatings, corporate goons, betrayals, and salvations. When the Blue Moon closed for the night, beer would be secured and a small hearty troop would repair to Iverson's flat-bottomed Skagit River tugboat, the *Ora Elwell*. Here the debates would rage for hours or days, sometimes punctuated with a refreshing swim in Lake Union, often ending with people sleeping all over the boat, from the pilot house to the old engine room. Amazingly, almost everyone was back at the Blue Moon by the afternoon.

As with so many other political movements Iverson was one of the first to tune in to the importance of women's liberation. In an era when self-conscious women were plugging up the Blue Moon's sewer system by flushing down their unwanted and now unfashionable bras, he was already keen on their issues. One day while holding forth with a crew of young radicals, the mother of his daughter happened to be strolling by the Blue Moon with a perambulator. She stopped, removed the infant's soiled diaper, went into the Moon, and clapped it onto his face. He got up, washed, and returned to resume his conversation as if nothing had happened. Iverson rarely missed a baby-sitting assignment after that.

Beneath his zany hats and layers of flannel shirts Iverson held forth, bringing together the various political and artistic radicals who called the Blue Moon home. Though a nonswimmer, one winter at two in the morning Iverson was leading a delegation to the *Ora Elwell* for another all-night discussion group when he gestured broadly and the momentum carried him off the dock and into the lake. There was so much air trapped beneath his various shirts that he bobbed right back up. A couple of stout fellows hauled him back up on the dock and he completed his philosophical point without apparent hiatus. He did note that this might obviate any immediate need for a bath. Snug aboard the *Ora Elwell* he could once again share more of his political experience and insight with the young radicals aboard with him. His embodied an idiosyncratic but very effective Socratic method.

One of the first calvings from the glacier created by the Cold War was the joint Apollo/Soyuz space mission in 1975. The space age was still wildly popular and had not become the quotidian hauling of equipment to outer space by astrophysicist teamsters that it has become today. People were still riveted to their television screens and their radios hanging on every word and deed from the heroic astronauts and cosmonauts hurtling a hundred or so miles above their heads around the globe. The symbolic uniting of the spacecraft from the United States and the former Soviet Union was more than high drama. In all this excitement the voices of the Russian cosmonauts could be heard throughout the English-speaking world due to the graceful and deft interpretation of the late Ross Lavroff. His musical-quality baritone—he also sang light opera—captured the voices and meaning of the cosmonauts as they and their American counterparts docked in space and brought the two nations together for the first time since World War II.

Ross Lavroff had fallen in love with Seattle when the army stationed him at Ft. Lewis near Tacoma, Washington. After his service he bounced around between Venice Beach, California, Stanley's Bar in New York City, and the Blue Moon Tavern in Seattle, working for the Voice of America, newspapers, and others requiring his Russian-language skills. Eventually he landed steady work with the State Department and other federal agencies, bought a houseboat on Lake Union a few blocks from the Blue Moon, and settled in. Although he specialized in the arcane terminology of military engineering, he also interpreted for fisheries, environmental issues, and business and social gatherings. At home he dressed like a sailor on shore leave, but once he put on his pinstripes it was all business. Mostly he tried not to work at home. He maintained an apartment in Geneva, Switzerland, for the duration of his work on the SALT I and II missile treaties. It was work he took great pride in.

On occasion, however, some of his responsibilities would spill over into Seattle. It was never a big surprise to see Lavroff at the tavern with two or three fisheries scientists and their KGB handler. For a time there was a picture of Leon Trotsky hanging on the ceiling over the tavern's entrance. He once brought a delegation of senior scientists to the Blue Moon for a beer and a chance to talk to local "normal" Americans. Upon seeing the Trotsky picture, some of the older scientists started giggling. Their young KGB officer, having never seen a picture of the assassinated former Bolshevik didn't know what to make of their mirth. No one told him. Lavroff said that eventually the fellow found out and was furious that he had been had like that. One of the Russian scientists confided in Lavroff that he thought that there might actually be more communists in the Blue Moon than there were in the Soviet Union. At one meeting in the Kremlin, upon being introduced to Mikhail S. Gorbachev, Lavroff was caught off guard when the former Soviet leader said, "From Seattle? How is the Blue Moon Tavern?"

Moonball is an institution unto itself. Twenty years ago the Blue Moon had a team in a coed tavern league. The Moon players were dismayed to learn that other teams featured all-male rosters and people who kept score and really cared if you were out or safe. Since the Moon team always had twenty to thirty people show up to play it dropped out of the league and started playing on its own. Every Sunday the Moonballers go out to a field and pick sides. There are an unlimited number of players on each side—the outfield is often very crowded—with people of all ages, abilities, and genders. There are no strikeouts, one must hit the ball with the bat and put it into play. (This is a popular feature for people who have not wasted their entire youth bringing bat and ball into intimate contact over and over again.) Sliding into base or knocking over beer cans are both against the rules as well as common sense. After fifteen to twenty innings victory is declared and those old enough repair to the tavern. The Blue Moon baseball season runs from Super bowl Sunday through the winter solstice, with a brief early-summer hiatus for camping up in the mountains.

Ray is a Moonballer. He is a slight Mexican-American with an engaging smile who restores houses for a living. His only regret is that when his family moved to the United States his father insisted that it would henceforth be an English-only household. "Man, if I'd've learned Spanish I'd be the foreman," he says with a laugh. His favorite night at the tavern is Opera Night on Mondays. Of course he also watches the broadcast of the local professional baseball team while the arias are being sung, smiling at the opera and sometimes hooting at the game.

Some other notables: Byron appears to be in his sixties, is unshaven, and has the indifference to his habiliments and hygiene that is natural to those who have chosen to live on the city streets. He can be seen walking almost any neighborhood in Seattle. Were he a star he would be of the seventh magnitude. He comes to the Blue Moon to drink coffee, talk to the musicians who hang out there, and engage in philosophical discussions with whoever is interested. Although he does not own a guitar, he is an excellent player with many fine stories about the greats and near-greats he has known. Often a young player will be sitting alone working on his guitar in the back of the tavern, and Byron will join him to share techniques and tales. His dental work, like Seattle's highway infrastructure, could use a little shoring up, but that doesn't prevent him from being a clear, concise, and engaging conversant.

Know anyone who has ever wanted to learn how to make an arrowhead? Kip is a flint knapper and can teach you how to make an atlatl from scratch, as well. Traffic bother you? Larry is a traffic engineer. Sylvia and Gary work at the Building Department. Andy retired from the gas company and can fix anything—including a cribbage game. Rebecca makes movies. Salem writes poetry and makes documentary films. Jack heads a genetic research team and plays keyboards in a rock band. Brandon is chief engineer on a fishing boat and can also fix anything, but he'll be gone for six months. Dave teaches math at the university and is a mountain climber. Dunny programs and repairs computers, designs Web sites, and although he has no legs, dances with the ladies while aboard his skateboard when there is live music. Marie is a graphic designer and her husband, Walt, writes history and runs the Historylink Web site. The Blue Moon is populated with an extraordinary variety of experts, all of whom are willing to share with those curious enough to ask. It has its zanies, too, but stars would lose something if they didn't twinkle.

Hank Reverman originally wanted to name the tavern the Big Dipper. However his soon-to-be partner Monty Fairchild already owned a café called the Blue Moon, and it was decided that it would be far less expensive to move the neon sign than make a new one. A great good place is a patchwork of people and whimsy, determination and luck. The walls of the Blue Moon have heard it all a thousand times, and will hear still more. No matter what their magnitude, the stars of the Big Dipper can yet be seen behind the well-worn glory of the bikini-clad lady lounging in the comforting arc of the Blue Moon. Whether the stars are new or old they will always be welcome in this unlikely great good place.

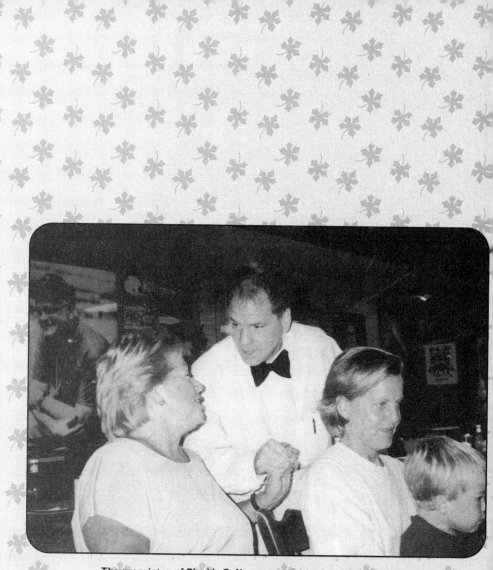

The proprietor of Plank's Café greets a visitor from County Cork, Ireland.

Plank's Café

COLUMBUS, OHIO

PLANK'S CAFÉ is familiar to me though I have not yet been able to visit it. It is the prewar, Midwestern version of the hospitable bar/restaurant around which so much community was built before community itself began to disappear in the onslaught of unifunctional zoning, the flight to neat and tidy but socially sterile suburbs, and the replacement of these kinds of places by impersonal chain operations.

In reading about Plank's Café, I was reminded of its counterpart in Mankato, Minnesota, which once had a lively downtown. Along Mankato's main shopping street was located near a German Rathskeller that my folks visited after shopping was done. There we all enjoyed an incredibly delicious wet beef sandwich on homemade bread. Mankato's downtown no longer exists. The mall up on the hill killed it. I hear that the local residents like their mall, and that's probably a good thing considering what they gave up for it.

More places like Plank's have disappeared than have survived. Fortunately for the people who derive so much enjoyment and social bonding from Plank's Café, two factors seem to have kept it alive since the Plank family took it over in the late thirties. First, the location has apparently not been targeted by any of the juggernaut chain operations that roll over the land cloning themselves wherever prospects look favorable. Second, successive generations of Planks have seen fit to carry on the tradition. If there is something like a *gemütlichkeit* gene running through some family lineages, the Plank family surely has it. There has been no waning of the vision and no flagging of devotion and effort evident as the third generation carries on.

When Nancy sent me her manuscript, she included some other materials about Plank's Café, and among them a letter from Frank Moskowitz, publisher of the *Buckeye Sports Bulletin*, which moves well at Plank's. Nancy apparently had asked him why he, personally, liked coming to Plank's. "It's because," he wrote, "the important and the not-so-important, the young and the old, Democrats and Republicans, etc., etc., can all mingle comfortably together." Many observers, and too often many planners, assume that a place like Plank's is a working-class phenomenon and that a more affluent middle class, and especially an upper-middle class, would not be found in such places. In point of fact, I doubt that one could find a more inclusive third place in this culture that now praises diversity.

In the late autumn of 1939, my father and mother bought the café at the corner of Parsons Avenue and Sycamore Street in Columbus, Ohio. It had originally opened in 1886 and went through a succession of owners as a saloon and restaurant until Prohibition, when it survived as an ice cream and soft drinks emporium.

When my father bought the café from his brother-in-law Ed Manns, he knew little about running a business and relied on the strong support of my mother to even give it a try. As a first generation German-American, he had been eking out a pretty miserable living for his wife and four children as a shoemaker. What he did have, and it was bred in his bones, was a love of people and a strong desire to have a good time. Depression days might have taken what money they made, but Dad and his friends managed to have their good times without money—just by being together.

Manns's café had afforded Dad and his friends many activities that came cheap: attending sporting events, playing cards, pitching horseshoes, planning picnics and other outings, and taking trips to Indian Lake. On occasion, Dad hosted home-brew parties in the cellar of our house. These experiences, in combination with his love of people, gave him what he needed to run a successful third place. He did it and did it well for twenty-one years, until his death from Hodgkin's disease in 1960.

On his deathbed, Dad encouraged my brothers, Walt and Willie, to buy Grundy's Bier Garten at Whittier and High Streets in Columbus. They did so the week of Dad's funeral and Willie left the original Plank's to take over Plank's Bier Garten, which he and his daughter, Chris, continue to operate into its fortieth year.

With Willie running the bier garten and Dad's brothers, who both participated in running the business, having passed away, Walt was running Plank's Café by himself. He was forced to close the place at 9:00 P.M. and business was floundering.

Walt decided to pass on Plank's Café to his son Tom, who attended Ohio State University in the sixties and who, having inherited the spirit of gemütlichkeit, made many friends there. Tom realized that his dad's place closed at the time of night when his friends were just getting started.

"First," Tom told me, "we moved closing back to ten, then eleven, then midnight. Finally, we stayed open as late as the law allowed, which was 2:30 A.M. Friday and Saturday nights." With Tom on the scene and closing time vastly extended, a major demographic shift took place. The customer base shifted from the old-timers of my grandfather's and father's time to a group ranging in age from late teens to early twenties.

The business soon came out of its slump. In fact, the place got so crowded that the fire marshal made them open a room upstairs. Many of Tom's friends became regulars and some of them, eventually, employees working alongside him. Older customers were not lost, however. The transition allowed Walt and his wife, Liz, to drop in during the evening after a show or a ball game, or to enjoy a round of cards. Their presence turned many casual customers into faithful friends.

ADAPTING TO CHANGE

I asked Tom how the older generation—the pillars of Plank's—reacted to the onslaught of teenagers in their midst. "No problem." Tom shrugged. "Guys like Carl Green entertained them. The two groups got a kick out of each other." How true that was. I can still see Carl sitting at his spot along the bar. He was a huge man with a big heart and a bold voice. Each time a familiar face came through the door, and that was almost everyone who came in, Carl set off a siren and a blinking red light that emanated from a hard hat he wore. He also had a knack for remembering everyone's birthday, the names of their relatives, and could always come up with an old, well-embellished story to keep them laughing.

I remember another of the old customers, a man in his eighties, nicknamed "Good Guy Jack" by the younger crowd. Jack brought apples, big red delicious apples, for the gang on weekends. The younger crowd looked forward to Jack's arrival and broke into a cheer when he made his appearance.

The older generation made the younger one feel accepted as adults, while the younger group fanned the sparks of youth in their elders. So what could have been a disadvantage turned out to be a satisfying exchange all around. Before long, the parents of many of Tom's younger friends began coming in on weekends and many of them remain loyal customers to this day.

Physical or architectural changes to Plank's were few but most of them were major. I have already mentioned opening a room upstairs to accommodate a growing clientele. That was minor. Early in 1950, and with Dad's approval, Walt tore down the wall that had divided the structure into bar and restaurant. The wall had served to keep women out of the bar as the "MEN ONLY" sign over the door indicated in the early days. This renovation surprised everyone—"Much bigger than I thought," Walt had said upon viewing its completion—and to this day, the room continues to serve the crowds adequately.

In 1972, Dad set Tom free to execute his idea of paneling all of the walls, upstairs and down, with barnwood siding. This would cover the aged plaster walls that were always in need of repair. Tom enlisted relatives, customers, and friends to scour farms for old barns and to pitch in to help him design and complete the job. The effect was both casual and warm.

The latest improvement began in 1989. Walt had dreamt of adding a room to double the capacity of the bar area and he took the occasion of Plank's fiftieth anniversary to implement the idea. It meant buying several adjacent properties and many in the building business, his own architect included, advised against it. Walt ignored all of them and proceeded methodically toward his goal. The café now stands as a monument to his keen vision and courage. The room is filled at lunchtime with workers from downtown offices and in the evenings with families and other groups—all as he had envisioned.

The menu, over the course of three generations, has expanded considerably. Wet beef, consisting of thin-sliced beef with homemade gravy over mashed or home fried potatoes, was the top menu choice for years. Then along came pizza to unseat the leader, though wet beef continues to be very popular. More recently tacos and chicken wings have been added along with club sandwiches and a greater variety of fish. Each day of the week has its special dish.

Drinking habits and tastes have changed less. Tom reports that regulars probably average four alcoholic drinks each, but that many do not drink alcoholic beverages at all. Some regulars, having given up the habit altogether, continue coming to Plank's for what it offers apart from alcohol. In my modest estimate, 99 percent of the appeal is conversation, which engages customers with other customers and with the bartenders; and should the customer be new or alone, with the waitresses as well.

The customer base changed, the fare changed, and the structure underwent physical change, but what is most important about Plank's is what did not change. Throughout the years, the integrity of Plank's has been maintained, which is to say that Walt's vision remained intact. The place has never tried to be anything but what it was. It may be more comfortable now, but the purpose it serves and its importance to the customers remains the same.

PLANK'S: THE INSTITUTION

a multitude of people, adults and children, rely on Plank's Café to host many events and interludes in their daily lives. Though many visits to the place are impromptu, many more are regular and ritualized, and some are even command appearances. Viewed from the inside, this institutionalization of hospitality is evident in the rhythms of the day, the week, and the year as played out at Plank's Café.

The 6:00 A.M. opening greets two or three judges from the downtown courthouse who start their day at Plank's. Since Willie's bier garten doesn't open early, eight to twelve of Willie's golfing buddies show up. Several people from the night shift at nearby hospitals come in for breakfast, though some of them prefer a pizza and a beer. Six or seven priests gather at Plank's on a weekly basis drawn by good food and camaraderie. Plank's advertises in many church bulletins.

St. Patrick's is the biggest day of the year for Plank's. The reveling starts early and goes on all day long. "Crazy Joe" entertains with music in the evening. All rooms, downstairs and up, are filled. Standing room only. Each year before the Ohio State–Michigan game in November, members of the OSU marching band and the OSU alumni band come one evening for a pep rally. Usually, some of the cheerleaders accompany them, which is always a big crowd pleaser. Afterward, the Plank family serves the band and the cheerleaders a dinner in the upstairs party room.

On Christmas Eve, families gather for early dinner. The place closes at 6:00 P.M. on that day. Throughout the day old friends gather to have a drink together. My nephew Tom adds that the night before Thanksgiving is a big night because the college gang has come home. They come to meet old friends before "being cooped up with family the next day."

In the summer, the softball teams gather at Plank's after their games. For several years, Plank's Café has sponsored between twenty-five and thirty teams that include softball, basketball, volleyball, golf, and bowling, buying uniforms and paying entry fees as required.

Coaches and teams gather to celebrate and to plan strategy. Grade school teams come on Saturdays and use Plank's for their awards banquets. High school teams come in after evening games. Coaches from all over town meet to exchange notes during the week, not just game night. As one of the regulars observed, "Plank's is truly a sports bar," meaning that sports is discussed intelligently in contrast to those places where multiple television sets do most of the talking.

On Monday Night Football evenings from September until mid-February, Plank's offers one-half off the price of all pizzas and a dollar off subs and chicken wings. Popcorn is always available and always free and the children like it because they are permitted to fill their own buckets. For in-town OSU games, Plank's hires a bus, serves a breakfast before departure, provides snacks on the bus, tailgate food and drinks, and returns to the café after the game.

RUNNING THE PLACE

The devotion to hospitality and inclusiveness found at Plank's is exceptional and, as you may already suspect, the owners and employees invest a great deal of themselves into making the place what it is. Walt's tradition is carried forth with effort and devotion, and it lives on in his three children, Tom, John, and Mary. The three of them present a nice composite of my brother's personality. In a strange and wonderful way, Walt is still there. Tom and Johnny spend an estimated eighty hours a week each behind the bar, according to Tom. Tom lives but three blocks away and, by choice, his total time in the café easily exceeds Johnny's. Tom says that things are best when his sister is there. Mary teaches second grade and opens the café at 6:00 A.M. on Saturdays. She works all day on Saturdays and full-time all summer. She says, "Sometimes I feel like Mother Theresa when I leave there after work." She resembles her father the most.

Every person who has entered into the spirit of the place remains there in one way or another. A staff of longtime employees offers support. Many have worked at Plank's for over fifteen years. Margaret Green, who began working at Plank's in January 1975, recently came to Tom and Johnny with tears in her eyes to tell them that her poor health and chronic lung weakness was forcing her to retire. Several others have reached the ten-year mark and still others are close behind. They consider themselves (and we consider them) part of our extended family.

One of the main obstacles in running the place today is finding and securing this kind of long-term and loyal help. Workers do not have the same attitude as the ones who have been there for many years. Many are recommended by customers, although that can be risky if it doesn't work out. The 5:00 P.M. to closing shift is the most difficult to fill. As to experience, Tom says some work out better if they've had no previous restaurant experience. Those with experience often "think they know, but don't."

How to keep good help? "Treat them right," says Tom. Lend them money when needed, "in a pinch." Take them to dinner at Christmas along with Tom's mother, his sister Mary, his wife Carol, and John's wife, Heidi. Give them a day's outing in the summer on Plank Island in Indian Lake. Take them to Scioto Downs to the races one or two nights a year. Give them OSU tickets from time to time. Buy them gifts.

If there is a secret to Plank's operation, it would be having a vigilant eye, an eye always alert to the customer who has not yet been greeted or the new one who needs to be introduced around and made to feel welcome.

Johnny considers this one of the most important aspects of his job. Everyone is made to feel welcome at Plank's.

The "problem" customer in the old saloon business was the unescorted female, so I asked Shirley, who has been a waitress there for fourteen years, about the comfort level of unescorted women. She laughed and told me that they are not harassed "unless they want to be." They are, she went on to explain, comfortable because they know the help and, usually, many of the customers. Invariably, they will see someone they went to school with or know through a friend. Tom contributes to the patrons' comfort, especially that of females, by disallowing foul language and offenders are asked to stop it or leave the premises.

REFLECTIONS

𝒶𝓂 I alone in longing for some sameness in life? I think not. Right about the time when I begin to have doubts, I see something in print—the great confirmer. In his final column in the November-December 1999 issue of *Modern Maturity*, Roger Rosenblatt wrote: " . . . change is good, exciting, and valuable. . . . The idea that there is something wonderful coming next is a great consolation."

But then he goes on to remind us that "of equal worth after age 50 are those aspects of life that do not change at all; that what is the best of next is often what was first, last, and forever adamant in its . . . silent efforts to hold fast against a culture that insists on nexts."

In the October 11, 1999, edition of *USA Today*, Alan Ehrenhalt brought it even closer to home in his article, "Don't Settle for Neighborhood Nostalgia." He extols the virtues of good old neighborhood gathering places such as grocery stores and drugstores, and he laments their passing. More than that, he reveals his repugnance for what he calls "franchised fiction," phony replacements for the real things. He looks forward to the day when we can have the old system back—"locally owned cafes, local food shops, even local convenience stores." All we have to do is spend our money in those few authentic places that have survived.

Ahh, that grand feeling of knowing I am not alone in my thinking. Others do share my longing for that sweet sensation of sameness. Thank you, Roger and Alan.

Plank's represents for me, as do other third places that I visit frequently, a refuge from a world that glorifies glitz and anoints newness for the sake of being new. It is rare, indeed, and it is extremely rewarding to be able to drop in and find friends anytime, day or night, all ages ready to make room for one more. Where, even if the place is almost empty around two in the afternoon, the walls seem to reach out and welcome you back.

People gather to watch Blues musicians play at the Juketown
Community Bandstand on Maxwell Street.

Maxwell Street

CHICAGO, ILLINOIS

WHY WOULD a third place that is doomed to extinction be included in a collection devoted to successes? Maxwell Street was a success for well over a hundred years and would continue to be but for the machinations of those for whom the robes of leadership are a poor fit. Maxwell Street did not fail as a third place; it succeeded mightily until done in by an institution of higher learning that will never offer half as much as it has taken away.

Maxwell Street was the model, par excellence, of what an urban, open-air market should be in a multi-ethnic, democratic society. It was a living and vibrant example of that harmonious diversity to which politicians and educators give lip service. It was an American dream realized.

I walked it on a warm autumn weekend of 1999 in the company of Steve Balkin, senior author of this chapter and one who had devoted countless hours and seemingly boundless energy in the attempt to save Maxwell. He introduced me to merchants and vendors, musicians and street characters amid the bustle of healthy street life. Although Chicago's leadership was claiming Maxwell Street to be the sort of place that is swarming with drunks and panhandlers, I encountered none of them the weekend I was there. I saw young black street vendors supporting their families by selling legal goods, not narcotics. Would they, I wondered, soon be reduced to a lesser livelihood?

Unlike the Biograph Theater which was within walking distance of Steve's home and which had merited an historic plaque, Maxwell had been awarded nothing. No plaque for the home of electric blues, of the zoot suit, the Ellis Island of America's second city. The leadership, I surmised, had taken care that nothing impede its plans to eliminate Maxwell and drive its inhabitants out to the remote suburbs.

Professor Balkin and Brian Mier inform us on the social and economic potential of open-air markets and alert us to what is likely to happen when the comfortable residents of a city take no interest in their less comfortable neighbors. My tour of Maxwell brought home what an acquaintance said with respect to his growing disenchantment with San Francisco: "The interesting people can't afford to live there anymore."

OUTDOOR MARKETS AS THIRD PLACES

Outdoor markets have been around since the beginning of recorded history. They are places where people go not only to buy and trade goods but to socialize, exchange news, and be entertained. Since outdoor markets are open to anyone, they have always been places where people from different walks of life can interact. They are usually the largest third places in towns and cities where they are located.

There are many stories throughout history that take place in markets. Plutarch, for example, writes about how Antony and Cleopatra disguised themselves as "commoners" and snuck into the market in Alexandria so they could interact with normal people. There have been many legendary markets throughout history. The famous ones, like Timbuktu and Samarkand, were always located at the hub of trade routes. Although it may be hard to believe for the average American today, there have been many famous open-air markets in the United States as well. Here is the story of one of the largest of these markets, Maxwell Street, which sat in Chicago, the air, trucking, and train hub of the United States. It was a market that regularly attracted crowds of 20,000 until the mayor, a group of real estate developers, and arrogant university bureaucrats decided to use public funds to build a suburban-style subdivision and some parking lots.

Maxwell Street was Chicago's oldest integrated neighborhood in the nation's most segregated city. Maxwell Street had an outdoor market since the 1870s, and for the last eighty years of its existence it was Chicago's official public market. For years it worked extraordinarily well as a third place, yet it will soon be destroyed despite an ardent movement to try to save it.

MAXWELL STREET AS A THIRD PLACE

Maxwell Street fulfilled the retail needs for Chicagoans just as shopping malls fulfill the retail needs of suburbanites. Unlike modern shopping malls, however, some of the market's other functions have disappeared from the contemporary retail experience. Maxwell Street was a place where Chicagoans could let their hair down, engage in revelry, socialize with old friends, meet people from other cultures, and make new friends. The experience of Maxwell Street was similar to that of markets around the world, whether in Africa, Asia, Europe, or Latin America.

Maxwell Street Market was created by immigrants to be an old-world oasis in modern urban Chicago. It served as both a commercial area and a residential neighborhood. Due to its similarity to old-world markets, its central location, and its aged buildings, it became a port of entry where recently arrived immigrants—first from Europe, then from the Deep South, and most recently from Latin America—could make money, find a cheap place to live, and meet people from their hometowns who welcomed them into informal support networks. It was a place where people would go to be entertained, even if they didn't have any shopping to do, by musicians who played on the street and invented a new American form of music called the electric blues. Musicians like Bo Diddley, Muddy Waters, and Howlin' Wolf got their start playing on Maxwell Street, and often continued to play there even after they became well known. It was a place where most people arrived on foot or by public transportation.

WHAT MADE MAXWELL STREET WORK

Maxwell Street was a weekly community festival where Chicago's poor and working-class people could find good cheap food and affordable merchandise, and listen to free live music. It was successful because it was convenient to get to, it had goods and services at modest prices, it acquired a tradition as a weekend destination–meeting place, and it was authentic. Because it was on public property, no one could be excluded and behavior was not managed. It was spontaneous and diverse, in a state of constant organic flux. People didn't know what to expect from week to week. It had a great location near downtown, just off a main thoroughfare near to the main train stations. Bordered by a retail district, churches, a wholesale produce market, and several ethnic neighborhoods, the neighborhood thrived, especially on weekends when the outdoor market occurred. There were a dozen hot dog stands that also served other foods like pork chops, and Polish sausages, filling the air with the smell of grilled onions. People would go to find low prices on second-hand goods and outdated clothing, and to hear blues musicians from the Deep South playing on street corners, in alleys and empty lots, and in taverns. Gospel groups were in abundance too. From the late 1800s to the 1920s, the neighborhood was predominantly Jewish. It had Sunday shopping when the rest of the city's stores were closed. Jewish merchants, who were discriminated against by mainstream white Gentiles, found it profitable to cater to poor and minority customers and to respect their culture. "The only color that matters is green" is a famous Maxwell Street saying.

The outdoor blues musicians and gospel singers were appreciated for drawing customers to the area—not scorned as nuisance street people to be arrested and removed. For over a hundred years, shoppers could count on getting good deals, meeting friends, and having fun. Its continuous year-round operation enabled people to observe and interact with each other over the span of several decades. This regular, casual interaction encouraged people to judge others based on their talents and character instead of stereotyping them by race and class. Over the years, shoppers and vendors could find people who had similar interests and learn who was trustworthy and who was not. This enabled friendships to blossom, money to be lent, business deals to be made, and start-ups to occur. One of the reasons poor people are poor is that their information networks are limited. People become confined to homogeneous neighborhoods where they hear the same information and meet the same kinds of people. Maxwell Street, by contrast, was a crossroads. It was ethnic neutral turf. It extended your social reach and the kinds of information that went with it.

On any given Sunday, up until the final days of the Market, there were over a thousand vendors. "If you can't find it on Maxwell Street," went one old saying, "you probably didn't need it"; "if somebody don't have it," went another, "they can get it for you." A motto of the market was "cheat you fair," which was a play on the phrase "treat you fair." This was old-fashioned, face-to-face, small-scale capitalism, imbued with the kind of playfulness that is still common in many countries around the world but is nowhere to be found in the modern shopping mall. There were many different kinds of vendors at Maxwell Street. Some, looking for a quick sale, would misrepresent their products as new when they were used, regular when they were irregular, working when broken, and correctly sized when they were ill fitting. If the customer was tricked during this kind of transaction, the vendor had "gotten one over" on him. But the customer had a chance. If the customer knew his stuff, he could find something that the vendor, through his ignorance, hadn't priced correctly and "get one over" on him. Furthermore, the customer could examine the merchandise and haggle over the price. More often than not, the customer did get a bargain because the sellers were very competitive, social relationships were established over time, and outdoor selling had little infrastructure, which kept costs down. In contrast, in contemporary corporate capitalism, the customer can be cheated unfairly. There is little chance to haggle and it is difficult to comparison shop and understand the fine print of contracts.

What Maxwell Street offered more than any contemporary shopping mall was spontaneity and freedom of expression. Commerce was conducted on the public streets. Anyone could come to start a business. Anyone could come and preach about religion, politics, or just bark out an ear-catching spiel to attract customers. Competitive capitalism reigned. If you were good at what you did, you succeeded. If you weren't, you failed, but the start-up cost was so low that you could try again until you found something that worked. Risk is the essence of entrepreneurship. People are willing to take on more risk when the cost of failure is low. This is something that supporters of a new poverty alleviation strategy called microenterprise development know about and encourage throughout the developing world and the United States, but that many shortsighted city officials who clamp down on street vending still can't seem to understand.

Maxwell Street was a real mosaic. Each group that lived in the neighborhood or frequented the market provided real-life lessons in multicultural awareness. It was a place where people could amuse themselves by simply sitting down under a tree or on a curb and chat with passersby. There were several cultural and ethnic enclaves in the market. Mexicans would congregate by the taco stands, Jews by the delicatessens, music lovers by the jam sessions, and jewelry traders by the jewelry tables. But there were few social boundaries. One could remain in one area for a while and then drift to another. This took place on public streets so no one could prevent anyone from going anywhere. There are many third places that, due to demographics in their surrounding neighborhood, cater to crowds that represent a narrow range of social class or ethnic groups, no matter how much more open they are than surrounding non–third place establishments. What made Maxwell Street unique is that it allowed people to socialize across an extremely wide range of racial and ethnic groups. Even during its final days in the 1990s, it was common to hear a score of different languages being spoken as one wandered through a crowd of 20,000 shoppers, from European languages like Polish, Lithuanian, Yiddish, Greek, and Spanish to Korean, Arabic, and Hausa. People who might greet you with suspicion in their own neighborhood would be friendly when meeting you on Maxwell Street. It was a business incubator where people could come for a second chance to climb the economic ladder through micro-entrepreneurship. On Maxwell Street, people could create something out of nothing. Newcomers could find mentors, informal capital, and a steady flow of customers.

HOW IT WAS DISMANTLED

University of Illinois at Chicago (UIC) has a history of insensitivity to its surrounding community. It was built in the 1960s during the reign of Mayor Richard J. Daley. During its construction, 8,000 people were forced out of their homes, the historic Jane Addams Hull House complex was destroyed, and the city was left with a cheap, sterile, tacky, fortress-like campus that looked like something a dinosaur coughed up after eating the United Nations Plaza. The campus design echoes what architect Victor Gruen, cited in Ray Oldenburg's book, called "civic centers that are concentration camps for bureaucrats, who are thus prevented from mingling with common folks."

The construction of the UIC campus is an example of growth politics. Growth machines were created after World War II through coalitions between the federal government, urban mayors, large institutions, and local real estate developers as a means to funnel federal funds into the inner cities. Growth machines promoted the razing of inner-city neigh-borhoods and dislocation of minorities in the name of "slum clearance" and their replacement with suburban-style developments that catered to middle-class whites. We agree with Ray Oldenburg's observation, "Segregation, isolation, compartmentalization, and sterilization seem to be the guiding principles of urban growth and urban renewal."

Eventually, federal funding to the old industrial cities began to dry up and local leaders were forced to come up with new growth strategies. In 1973 a group of private real estate developers came up with a plan called Chicago 21 that was endorsed by Mayor Daley. The plan aimed to use a combination of public and private sector money to expand the city's downtown central district. In order to sell the downtown area to the pri-vate sector, the plan called for the replacement of the poor African-American and Hispanic neighborhoods that bordered downtown with upscale market housing. During the 1980s, the Harold Washington admin-istration countered with a more inclusive development plan that aimed to minimize displacement of residents, but after Washington's death, Mayor Richard M. Daley (Richard J. Daley's son) reinstated Chicago 21 with the help of the original developers. Today, Maxwell Street is one of the last minority neighborhoods within the boundaries of the original plan.

In the early 1990s UIC decided to expand south into the Maxwell Street neighborhood, ignoring the more logical western direction that would have connected it with their medical center. There were people with political clout who did not want their homes and churches destroyed in this between-the-campuses Italian neighborhood, so they encouraged UIC to move south instead, in the neighborhood of people with the least resources to defend themselves.

In 1993, the city and UIC announced their intention to shut down the market. In early 1994, the city sold most of the land upon which the mar-ket stood to the university. A group called the Maxwell Street Coalition was formed to try to save the market.

Although UIC had a bad record on community issues, there was evi-dence that things were improving. Starting in the late 1970s, factions within the university had successfully worked with community organi-zations to minimize the kind of displacement typically associated with the growth machine. By the early 1990s, several members of UIC's planning department had published articles on battling the growth machine. A think tank called Great Cities, which aimed to promote the inclusion of neighborhood residents in the development process, was set up on campus. Therefore, the Maxwell Street Coalition had reason to believe that it would receive some support from the Great Cities program and members of UIC's urban planning department. This did not prove to be the case. Regimes change. The director of the Great Cities Institute publicly supported the elimination of the market and the razing of the neighborhood. Only two professors in the urban planning department worked to help the coalition.

In September 1994 the city created an alternative market on an empty street that had no storefronts for musicians to plug their instruments into, and vendor fees increased five thousand percent. Due to the city's oppressive new regulatory structure and fee increase, eight hundred Maxwell Street vendors were immediately forced out of business. Today, while worth a visit, the new Maxwell Street Market looks more like a typical midwestern flea market. A large portion of the vendors at the new market never sold at the old one. Still, UIC touts it as a success story that shows how they "saved" Maxwell Street.

As a result of UIC's initial southward expansion plan, several blocks of residential and retail units were destroyed, and hundreds of minority residents and dozens of businesses were displaced. Although every other neighborhood within a few miles of Chicago's downtown area is booming, Maxwell Street has lost hundreds of jobs and the city lost millions in tax revenue due to people's fear that if they invest in the neighborhood, their property will be seized and destroyed by UIC.

Meanwhile, the remaining businesses continue to serve the retail needs and provide third places for a predominantly African-American and Hispanic shopping community. Still, the neighborhood artificially appears decrepit because UIC purchased about 40 percent of the remaining buildings, evicted the tenants and let the buildings sit vacant and in disrepair. Despite complaints by neighborhood residents, UIC is lax in boarding up the backs of their buildings. Subsequently, several historic structures have been destroyed by fire.

By failing to maintain its vacant buildings, UIC succeeded in creating an appearance of blight in the neighborhood. The city aided UIC by neglecting its garbage collection service. This enabled UIC to qualify the neighborhood for Tax Increment Financing (TIF), an urban public finance arrangement that encourages gentrification and displacement. Mayor Richard M. Daley uses TIF as his primary development tool. With TIF, the city is able to issue bonds to finance construction, which are to be paid back over the course of decades through increases in real estate taxes. When UIC decided to expand its campus into the Maxwell Street neighborhood, the city awarded it with $55 million in TIF. This gave UIC the power of eminent domain to seize control of and demolish all buildings in the neighborhood and enabled it to become partners with private developers to construct luxury town houses on half the campus expansion land.

In the fall of 1997, UIC and the Chicago Department of Planning released their new South Campus Expansion Plan. According to the plan, the neighborhood would be completely razed and replaced with parks, a performing arts center, dormitory housing, and an 855-unit luxury subdivision. A series of protests were initiated against the TIF. Blues legend Jimmie Lee Robinson issued a Maxwell Street Blues CD and summed up his position in a song called "Maxwell Street Tear Down Blues" when he sings "Since you've started with that damn wrecking ball, our lives, our dreams, our needs continue to fall. The great history of this area which once stood proud and tall, guess what UIC, you've managed to destroy it all."

UIC argued that the buildings and businesses were not worthy of historic preservation. They supported this with the fact that the Illinois Historic Preservation Agency refused to designate the area as a historic landmark. The Illinois Historic Sites Advisory Committee unanimously voted to put the area on the National Register of Historic Places but it was vetoed at the top of the agency. UIC's public relations department failed to mention, however, that the wives of two of UIC's real estate developer partners sat on its board of directors.

At the city's public TIF hearings, UIC administrators used the same rhetoric that it has always used against people who try to preserve third places. They said coalition members were "anti-development," wanting to "hold back job creation," and were "absolutely insane." None of them mentioned the hundreds of jobs, businesses, and property tax revenue that had disappeared as a result of UIC's land banking. The city read off a long list of community organizations that supported South Campus expansion. Every one of these groups did business with the city or UIC.

The TIF was pushed through the city council without any dissent. Six years after demolition of most of the neighborhood, nothing has been built except for some perpetually empty parking lots and a few ball fields, which are the minimum structures that the city code requires for a public institution to build on vacant land. The destruction here is a classic example of Ray Oldenburg's observation, "One of the oft-repeated tragedies of the times is that white urban planners remove these important settings from the neighborhoods of the have-nots of society and can only imagine that they have done the people a favor."

THE MOVEMENT TO SAVE MAXWELL STREET

In 1993, the director of the Levine Hillel Center at UIC, Elliot Zashin, held a public symposium about Maxwell Street and invited scholars from all over the city to speak. Zashin, besides being a Jewish educator, was a political scientist. He was intellectually curious about this old neighborhood, with Jewish roots, that bordered on UIC. The symposium was the first time many of us found others who were similarly impressed with the history and function of Maxwell Street. At a reception after the symposium a group of kindred spirits decided to organize to try to stop the destruction of this neighborhood. Many of us were especially incensed by a UIC administrator who said at the symposium that he was not going to consider any points that had been made and would continue to push for complete destruction of the neighborhood.

The group named itself the Maxwell Street Coalition and used the Levine Hillel Center and a community development corporation in the nearby Mexican Pilsen neighborhood for meetings and to seek funding. Many Pilsen residents feel that UIC's encroachment in nearby Maxwell Street will accelerate gentrification (higher rents, higher taxes, and the accompanying displacement) in Pilsen as well. This fear is based on UIC's collaboration with private developers to build luxury town houses on its border. The current UIC campus was built on top of the first Mexican immigrant neighborhood in Chicago. After they were forced out of their homes by UIC in the 1960s, many of them migrated to the nearby Pilsen neighborhood. Mexican-Americans in Chicago put down strong social roots in Pilsen that they don't want to lose. Many feel that destroying Maxwell Street will be the first step toward a second displacement of the Mexican community.

The coalition formed committees to place the area on the National Register of Historic Places, to develop win-win alternative campus expansion plans allowing both UIC and the market to share the neighborhood, to lobby politicians, testify in City Council and write editorials, and hire an organizer to put together a vendors association. The university, with its immense financial resources (annual budget of a billion dollars), PR staff, patronage army, lobbying apparatus, alumni networks, and mayoral backing, aborted our every effort. We were part-time volunteers and they had full-time staff. With over a thousand college faculty and prominent departments in urban planning, social work, anthropology, sociology, and architecture, only three of the faculty gave us any assistance or spoke out against UIC's old-fashioned, urban renewal people removal policy. UIC faculty's politically correct liberal rhetoric turned out to be just empty posturing. Most of the faculty had never even visited Maxwell Street. They would drive past on their way someplace else and see a multitude of poor, minority, mostly male street vendors and shoppers and stereotype them as criminals. Owing to its long multicultural history, the reality was that the area was safer than most inner-city neighborhoods in Chicago. On a typical Sunday, with over 20,000 shoppers and 1,200 vendors, only two police officers were necessary to police the entire market. UIC administrators asked me, "would you want your [white] daughter to walk through Maxwell Street on her way to classes?" Statistically speaking, she was safer from an implied potential rape at Maxwell Street than she would have been on UIC's campus.

THE BLUES STRATEGY

Americans generally don't read. For people to learn about their history, it has to be embodied in a bricks and mortar historic district. Without a historic district, the stories of old Maxwell Street will be forgotten within a couple of generations. America may not always be at the top of the global economy and may again need to know how to create something from nothing. Furthermore, in the late 1990s, the coalition felt it was time for racial and class segregation in Chicago to end. An out-of-state politician gave us sobering advice. He told us to stop talking about Maxwell Street as a place that helps poor people because in America most of the public don't care about the poor. He asked if there was anything cultural about the place that we could get support for. That was why we switched the emphasis to blues history. The coalition had emphasized Maxwell Street's music history but now it took center stage.

Maxwell Street was one of the places where urban electrified blues was created. When blues musicians from the Deep South came to Chicago as part of the Great Migration, many of them started out in the Maxwell Street neighborhood. It was an easy walk from the Illinois Central railroad station, and cheap housing could be found. Eastern European Jews who lived and worked in the area were less prejudiced than other ethnic groups in the city. Since the Jews themselves were discriminated against, they welcomed the southern African-Americans as customers. It was a great contrast to the discrimination African-Americans experienced in the Deep South or in other ethnic neighborhoods in Chicago. I heard one Jewish businessman in the area say that when he heard musicians singing blues in a minor key, it sounded like a cantor in a synagogue.

Newly arrived musicians could immediately make money playing on Maxwell Street. They would perform on street corners, in empty lots and alleys, at parties and at taverns. They did not need an agent, a union card, or a new suit of clothes. All they needed was a place to plug in their electric guitars and amplifiers. Musicians listened to each other, bands formed, and information about jobs was circulated. What was particularly thrilling was that musicians from the audience were invited to sit in. Many a blues musician learned to play from watching and sitting in on Maxwell Street. The type of blues created on Maxwell Street in the 1940s and 1950s—Chicago-style blues—was the root music of rock and roll. Prior to this, blues was mainly a rural and an acoustic music. Here it had become an urban and an electrified music.

The Coalition raised awareness of Maxwell Street's blues significance and received support from blues and rock fans from all over the world. Several blues jam session protests were held, but in general the local blues establishment snubbed us. Few wanted to back a cause that did not have the endorsement of the mayor, as he gave subsidies to favored organizations and ran the annual Chicago Blues Festival. One alderman on the South Side even told city hall she did not want any other neighborhood to have an historic blues district because she wanted to create one and didn't want any competition.

In 1994, UIC and the city destroyed most of the buildings in the old market area and eliminated the historic market. However, after 1994, there were still sixty old buildings remaining, most with businesses still in them, including three hot dog stands. Those hot dog stands were the anchor businesses of the area, the core third places, which Ray Oldenburg defines as: "the place where one is more likely than anywhere else to encounter any given resident of the community."

One of the hot dog stands has been in its same location since 1911 and invented the Maxwell Street polish sausage, a Chicago street food staple that is served in most independent fast food restaurants in the city. Minorities and working class people continued to visit the hot dog stands from all over the city. Hanging out here, one would hear gossip from Mississippi and Mexico and see Gypsies, Hispanics, African-Americans, truck drivers, cops, and construction workers of all nationalities eating together. One would see UIC students but never a UIC professor or administrator, even though Maxwell Street was just a couple of blocks away from the main campus. UIC faculty and administrators had disdain for these people and did not want to see the faces and culture they were about to eliminate. For them, ignorance was bliss. The Coalition offered to take several UIC administrators on tours, including the famous postmodern scholar of multiculturalism, Stanley Fish. All refused.

The area had over a hundred years of tradition. Besides the hot dog stands, there were specialty clothiers and inexpensive tailors. The zoot suit was invented on Maxwell Street and several stores still sold them. About thirty street vendors who sold in the old market continued to sell socks, hats, dish towels, perfume, and T-shirts. They called themselves hustlers. We call them entrepreneurs. They were doing what they were supposed to be doing: earning an honest living and engaging in boot-strap capitalism. UIC taught entrepreneurship but the university and its entrepreneurship center had no interest in helping these people. Instead, UIC wanted to drive them out of business.

A reconstituted coalition was formed in 1995 to save these remnants of old Maxwell Street. The Maxwell Street Historic Preservation Coalition wanted to save as many of the remaining sixty buildings as possible, allow the businesses to remain for those who still wanted to stay in the area even though they would likely pay higher rents and taxes, and to insure afford-able housing was provided for the remaining residents. Inspiration came from a visiting historic preservation specialist from Memphis who told the coalition about Beale Street, a similar street in Memphis. Memphis saved the last few blocks of Beale Street and it has become a new music-based entertainment district—the number one tourist attraction in Memphis. "Maxwell Street has more buildings and they are in better shape than in Beale Street and the coalition should do whatever it could to save the district. It is an American heritage treasure," she said.

One of the first things the newly reconstituted coalition did was set up a Web site to disseminate information on the cultural and historic value of Maxwell Street. It was thought there would be a compelling and prof-itable reason for UIC to save the area. While there was some interest with-in the university in doing this, the vice chancellor who backed our posi-tion was fired, so Mayor Daley's handpicked real estate developers and UIC's administrative staff could now call the shots. UIC had to make a token gesture, so the head of the City Department of Planning and the developers came up with a plan to temporarily save eight buildings (none from Maxwell Street itself) and thirteen facades to be pasted on a new Maxwell Street parking structure. Maxwell Street was not UIC's preferred place for a parking structure, but placing it there gave them a rationale to destroy the remaining buildings. As things stand today, no whole building will remain on Maxwell Street. UIC plans call for evicting the remaining businesses and leaving the area fallow for a few years to make sure none of the poor and minority people come around again. They don't want poor people socializing and shopping in the neighborhood because they are concerned it might lower the value of their luxury town houses and might frighten parents of students from the suburbs.

Maxwell Street was a successful third place in terms of its longevity and the good it did by helping people start businesses, allowing people to socialize across race and class, creating new cultural art forms, and providing opportunities to enhance the lives of the poor. It was such a special place that a movement emerged to try to keep it going and to at least preserve its memory so places like it would get more respect and reverence instead of being treated as a problem to eliminate. But classism and racism are so entrenched in the government of Chicago and its main public university that the war seems lost. It can only be hoped that the trail of debate and documentation left by this battle will ensure that what happened to Maxwell Street will never happen again to other similar areas.

A regular at the Coffee Beanery gives an impromptu speech
during one of Marsha Alfafara's classes.

The Coffee Beanery

ROCHESTER, MICHIGAN

COMMUNICATION 220—It's the only Oakland University course listed in the Coffee Beanery's monthly calendar of events. It's the only public speaking class with built-in visual and auditory hurdles—students vie for audience attention near a glowing neon coffee cup, against a bustling Main Street backdrop and over the occasional din of whirring espresso maker, ice-crunching blender and coffeehouse chit-chat.*

As Mike Ryoko's generation of journalists knew, a third place is a classroom wherein everyone learns a little bit about a lot of things and a lot about human nature. Here, however, Marsha Alfafara moves beyond the metaphorical and teaches an actual university course in communication in a third place called the Coffee Beanery, located near her home in Rochester, Michigan.

Professor Alfafara takes us along as she and the third place work their magic on a new class of students in this unconventional setting. Rarely does one observe the growth and development of students in a single course as one does here, and it is in the areas of citizenship and democratic participation that their growth is most obvious.

Back in the 1920s, when independent retailers fought and lost their battle against the chain stores, one of their arguments was that the chains would reduce citizens to consumers. We now have a better understanding of the truth in that argument. Citizenship's debt to third place association is substantial, as Professor Alfafara's account attests.

When **I was** offered the opportunity to teach COM 220—Public Talk on Public Issues, I had only one stipulation—that I

---

* Dargay, S. (1998, April 19). Coffee-klatching 220. *Clarion-Eccentric*, pp. A1, A3.

teach it in a public place. The choice of place was easy . . . The Coffee Beanery in downtown Rochester, Michigan.

My *third place.*

Exactly two city blocks from my front door, the Beanery is my home away from home. The floors are scuffed, the chairs are hard, and the roof leaks. The walls are decorated with the work of local artists, promoting their talent. I can walk in at any given time of day and I am sure to meet someone I know. It may be a neighbor, a student, the mayor, or a Leader Dog, its trainer, and trainee.[**]

I started hanging out at the Beanery several years ago when I ran my business from my home. Sometimes, I just needed a break from my office. It's funny how things work out; in seeking a break from my home office I found a home away from home. I also found something else, something that gives meaning to my life and allows me to bring all that I value together under one roof.

More than anything, I value people. Family, friends, students—I don't make a distinction as roles often merge. Following closely behind is community, as it is where we meet people. Third, I value teaching and learning—again I don't make a distinction as the roles blur. In the classroom, as in life, we are simultaneously teachers and learners. I have the unique opportunity to teach what I practice.

LESSONS TAUGHT

COM 220 is based on the ideas that public speaking is an interdependent process and everyone can be an effective public speaker. The keys are knowledge and incentive.

Together, knowledge and incentive can create a "gift" an individual can give to his or her community—a voice. The use of a public voice creates "giftedness," the sharing of an individual's skills, talents, knowledge,

---

[**]Rochester, Michigan is the home of Leader Dogs for the Blind, "a non-profit group that is committed to provide the legally blind with a means to help them live a better life." http://leaderdog.org/main.html Training takes place throughout the community.

and community experience, which encourages positive interaction and promotes cultural growth and community bonds.

COM 220 teaches students that speaking publicly about real issues helps cultivate community. For our purposes, the community is the geographical location where one resides and works. Within communities are areas of free association where people meet and engage in conversation, shoot the breeze, gossip, and enjoy good old idle talk. Areas of free association as described by Ray Oldenburg are third places.

Moving off campus emphasizes this concept of third places and helps foster understanding of how one's voice builds community. In the beginning, students are assigned speeches that encourage self-reflection. These speeches assist students in understanding the personal "gifts" they have to share. As the individual's understanding of his or her personal gifts grows, and when combined with knowledge of community, its members, and needs, incentive is inspired. Students are directed not only to attend speeches at the Beanery, but also to seek out third places within their respective communities where they are to communicate with the regulars, learn about issues of interest within their community, and then discuss in class what they learn. Once they are equipped with knowledge and incentive, students seek issues of interest within their respective communities that they can address. For their final speech assignment, students speak on these issues within their communities.

TUESDAY NIGHT AT THE BEANERY

To me, the move to the Beanery is a natural choice; to my students . . . well, it is an adjustment.

"You want us to do what?" is usually the initial response.

Taking a public speaking class "in public" is a bit frightening for them, but they soon warm to the idea of not having to scramble for parking on campus. Plus, they love the thought of having coffee readily available.

In a recent session, the first class at the Beanery was a bit chaotic. We literally took over the place. Coffee Beanery staffers Tim and Jaclyn were kept busy behind the counter taking orders for cappuccino and lattes.

Finally, after some discussion, we settled on a seating arrangement in which we could all see one another—quite a task with seventeen of us. Once we settled in, I welcomed the class to my third place and, like a proud parent, introduced the class to the regulars who had assembled to greet them. Among the "regulars" that evening were Don, Sue, daughters Anna and baby Beth, and my neighbor Alice.

At one time, I had my doubts about taking the class off campus and teaching it in this manner, but no longer. You can teach "concepts," but to truly understand the value of public speech, it must be experienced. The jovial, relaxed environment of the Beanery lends itself to that experience, which encourages learning.

For our group, it wasn't long before the students grew comfortable in their new environment. As their confidence grew they began to speak. Oh, so eloquently they spoke!

SMALL STEPS

The first assignment was to introduce a reading, recite it, and then interpret it. The selections were as diverse as the speakers, from Eastern philosophy to Winnie the Pooh, from Led Zeppelin to letters from a friend. The last was read by an Israeli student who shared the words of a friend whose life came to tragic end in a military conflict. By evening's end there was not a dry eye in the house.

With each selection, students shared their lives and gave meaning to ours.

The next assignment was a considerably lighter topic—joy. I instructed students to reflect on what joy is, what they do to find inner peace and joy, and how they renew themselves. Students immediately questioned the limits on the subject matter. They were told as long as they did not break any rules of the university, the sky was the limit . . . come share your joy.

And they did, sharing sight, sound, playfulness, and spirit.

Together we touched our inner-children as we finger-painted on a poster board that was later displayed on the walls. We blew soap bubbles and let our cares float away. We sang in harmony and let music fill our soul. We watched spellbound at one student's joy of performance as

Hamlet, pondering life's greatest questions, came to life before our eyes. One of the regulars commented: "I have paid seventy-five dollars a pop for lesser performances, and all I had to do for this was to order coffee."

A BIG STEP

The last assignment for the Beanery course was that the students present an individual philosophy of life. At first, many students protested that they did not have a personal philosophy. I granted that this is a difficult speech to give. It requires digging deep inside and recognizing what it is that moves us. It requires not only reflection on what words we live by but the sharing of those words with others. It is a public confirmation of self.

This speech, more than any other, involved the most personal risk. After several weeks of class and inside the now safe, comfortable environment of the Beanery, however, it was a risk the students could take. Fortunately, the students had come to see this third place as a secure, friendly environment, which enabled them to share a deeper understanding of themselves. We heard about faith in God, belief in the Golden Rule, and of balance and harmony. We heard of turning the other cheek, of the strength to "keep on trying."

As motivating as these speeches were to the audience, they were even more confirming to the speaker. As one student noted, "I have thought those words many times. It was not until tonight that I believed them."

OUT AND ABOUT

As the semester progressed students were directed to seek out third places within their own communities; it is here that I met with the most skepticism. They refused to accept they could be noticed and welcomed within their own communities—not to mention valued.

It was awkward for them at first. They received guidelines—go at the same time each week, sit in the same place, order the same thing, listen to folks and talk to them. It is, after all, a communication class. They joked that they had never before been assigned to eavesdrop and that Mom taught them never to talk to strangers.

At first they came back with stories of the folks they observed and those who had observed them. They identified those they encountered with such titles as the "clown," for a woman who in the judgment of the student wore excessive makeup; the "group of seniors"; the "yuppie couple"; and the exhibitionist at a health club. They noticed that they attracted the attention of individuals within their environment. They learned that friendly smiles promoted a response.

FITTING IN

By midsemester the students were surprised that they were becoming regulars in their third places. They no longer had to ask to be served but were greeted with, "The usual?" If they missed a week, their absence was noted. They became part of their third places, not just observers. The yuppie couple was now Todd and Barbara. The seniors were crossing guards for the local elementary school.

Something else started to happen as the semester progressed—students started getting to the Coffee Beanery before me. Tardiness was rare. Often I would be greeted by Tim or Jaclyn with the words, "Marsh, one of your students called. They are running late but will be here."

Another interesting thing happened: I no longer had to prompt discussions.

Open forum, a portion of the class set aside allowing students to discuss encounters in their own third places, would be started by students with comments like, "Kurt, how is the war going between the snowboarders and skiers?" or "Stan, what did the cops at Big Boy think of . . ." or "Hey, Melanie, is that guy still checking you out?" and "The clown spoke to me."

Open forum became livelier as we learned about the characters in each other's third places. It was as if we knew them. As we learned more about them, we learned about their likes and issues of concern.

And, as expected, the more the students learned about their communities the more they invested themselves. They were becoming a more informed public and they wanted to share. Our open forum at the Beanery became open to *everyone*, as it should be. It was not unusual to find family members, friends, council members, journalists, or musicians showing up at class. According to the local press, "It's the easiest course to unofficially audit."

During open forum all were given an equal opportunity and encouraged to speak. Students took notice of one another and their guests. Those who appeared too timid were warmly encouraged. Those who came to lecture were sanctioned. Fond memories of open forum include the night a local political figure came to speak on an issue dear to his heart. He was truly welcomed as an equal by his constituency when "his" issue was given no greater weight then local gossip. Another memory is when Alice, who professed she never could speak in public, told of winning a medal in the Special Olympics.

Once the pattern of reporting on people and happenings in individual third places was established, open forum could easily run the entire evening. There was more to this course than open forum, though, and in order to allow time for speeches I had to limit it to no more than half the class period. The students understood the necessity of limiting time, but they brooded about it anyway. Finally, they took the initiative and started their own tradition, establishing their own third place closer to campus where they would meet after class.

What a ripple effect third places have.

THE LEAP

Now that they had learned more about themselves, it was time for the students to share their gifts not just with classmates but also with their communities. The final speech for this class was not given in a third place.

Students were assigned to speak in their own community on issues of importance after gathering information in their third place. The issues and locations of the speeches were as varied as the climates of their individual environments. Pam addressed the Senior Center and brought the house down speaking on the importance of humor in daily life. Nirva spoke on the rewards of volunteerism to student organizations. Ido spoke to students at the Jewish Community Center on what it was like being raised on a communal farm in Israel.

Even with the preparations they had gone through, it still required courage to stand before an audience and give a speech. Once class member, Stan, was surprised with a little larger audience than he expected. The night of our class he was scheduled to speak on the good works of a patrol officer, a regular from his third place, at a local council meeting. The class decided to move to the township hall and lend Stan its support.

Stan praised the officer who has worked with the local youth in his community. His speech was well received, not just by the council but by many of the regulars from Stan's third place, mostly policemen and firefighters, who were in attendance. His speech was even mentioned in the local paper.

The speech yielded several added bonuses. First, as the township office is adjacent to the fire station, the class was invited for a tour after the meeting. The diverse class of undergraduates, graduates, students, and professionals had a wonderful time. There's nothing like watching a bank president in a full business suit sitting in the driver's seat of a fire truck. For this class, sharing our gifts is what community is all about. In this case, the community shared back.

There was one more special bonus. Shortly after the speech, the officer that Stan praised was given a promotion. He later told Stan that he believes it was the presentation before the council that brought his work to the attention of his superiors.

LESSONS INCORPORATED

Toward the end of the semester the students had become Tuesday night regulars at the Coffee Beanery. Speeches and open forums were effortless, like conversations among longtime friends. Anna and baby Beth were passed from one person to another. Nonregistered "students" would show up prepared to deliver assigned speeches. The only thing that separated "original" students from those "auditing" the class were the names on a class list.

By becoming regulars at the Beanery, the students came to realize the importance of third places and started incorporating them into their lives. Students who had once said to me they "could not possibly find time" for the third place assignment, were saying the at end of the semester, "I stopped by twice last week."

They learned that through our interaction with one another we gain meaning in our lives. We find out who we are.

A former student put it well: "Due to my husband's work, we had to relocate. The first thing I did in our new town was to seek out a third place. With so much change in my life I did not want to lose *me*. I knew I would find myself with the help of a third place. I did."

Through third places, we gain a greater understanding of what we have to offer. Recently, another student told me she has decided to run for public office, something she never thought she would have had the ability to do.

It was her third place friends who encouraged her.

I think my teaching assistant Stephanie sums it up best, though. "It is not that the students didn't understand the concept of third places. Without experiencing one, they did not see the value. They did not see their own personal value."

The third place is a learning place.

Acknowledgments

I **must first** of all thank the contributors to this collection. It has been a pleasure to have known and worked with people who have done so much for their communities at a time when community is so elusive in our society.

My gratitude goes to a multitude of journalists, reviewers, and associations that have sustained interest in the "third place" concept since the first book appeared in 1989. It was the durability of the concept and its continuing relevance to our culture that encouraged this project.

I am especially indebted to Matthew Lore, who took charge of the first book after Marlowe acquired it and who crafted the second and third editions, giving *The Great Good Place* new life. Matthew encouraged this companion volume and I have greatly enjoyed working with him. One could not ask for a more polite and considerate editor. That Matthew has his own third place undoubtedly lent much to our relationship.

Finally, I am deeply appreciative of the efforts of Suzanne McCloskey, who took over the project upon Matthew's elevation in the ranks. There were many loose ends, incomplete submissions, late additions, and so forth, which she handled deftly and promptly. The skill and professionalism of Matthew and Suzanne have made a difficult undertaking seem easy.

About the Contributors

Marsha Alfafara is a special lecturer in communication at Oakland University in Rochester, Michigan, and the president of Praxis Communications, a company whose mission is to create and support programs of community integration and inclusion. In her spare time she hangs out at the Coffee Beanery.

Peter Apanel is best known as the creator of the Pasadena Doo Dah Parade in 1977, which he ran for eighteen years. In 1995 he became involved in the development of the Arts Colony in Pomona, California, where he helped create by design what normally takes place by accident in downtown revitalization.

Steve Balkin is a professor of economics at Roosevelt University in Chicago. His grandfather Nathan was a horse wagon junk peddler who frequently socialized on Maxwell Street. Balkin cofounded and operates the Web site Openair Market Net, which focuses on outdoor markets all over the world. Balkin served with co-contributor Brian Mier on the board of directors of the Maxwell Street Historic Preservation Coalition. He lives in Chicago.

Larry Bourgeois is the director of Old St. George in Cincinnati, Ohio. He has been deeply interested in "third places" since his teens and has been captivated by the American coffeehouse movement since the 1960s. For the past twenty-five years he has operated bookstores and founded bookstore/coffeehouses and great good places.

Lynne Breaux is a native New Orleanian and former model with over thirty years' experience in the hospitality industry. She moved to Washington, D.C., in 1984 and purchased Tunnicliff's four years later. In addition to being Tunnicliff's proprietress, Breaux is a mother, a board member of both the Restaurant Association of Metropolitan Washington and the National Licensed Beverage Association, and a Capitol Hill cheerleader.

Annie Cheatham is the founder and owner of Annie's Garden and Gift Store in Amherst, Massachusetts, and has established other third places in the U.S. Congress (the Congressional ClearingHouse of the Future) and at Taipei American School. Co-author of *This Way Daybreak Comes: Women's Values and the Future*, Cheatham is also an educator, artist, and host of the weekly talk show *The Backyard Gardener*.

Patrick J. Devine, Ph.D., is associate professor of sports psychology at Kennesaw State University, near Atlanta. He consults with professional and amateur athletes and sports teams.

Richard Futrell has been the proprietor of the Third Place coffeehouse since the mid-1990s. His lifelong interest in social behavior has prompted him to travel the world extensively, always on the lookout for other third place settings.

Charles John Gourgott, M.D., a board certified ophthalmologist and former research physician, is the technical and medical consultant for World Gym International, based in Santa Monica, California. He is a former world-class Olympic weight lifter and the winner of numerous physique contests.

Gustav Helthaler, Jr., was born in Germany and raised in Detroit, where he studied and worked briefly as a tool designer. He settled in Seattle in 1970 and has co-owned the Blue Moon Tavern for the past twenty years.

Bob Holcepl worked as a photographer for over twenty years, winning numerous professional awards and seeing his work made part of the Cleveland Museum of Art's permanent collection before leaving photography to open a café in a transitional neighborhood with his wife, Nancy. Holcepl lives with his wife and daughter in Cleveland.

Theo Karantsalis, a trained Immigration and Customs official, has participated in many successful business ventures, including the establishment of the Miami Passport Photo Shop. He and his family live in Miami Springs, Florida.

Nancy Plank Kelley has expressed her passion and appreciation for third places by documenting the history of her family's restaurant, Plank's Café. A wife and mother of seven, Kelley lives in Columbus, Ohio.

Paul LaPorte makes his living writing for technology-based client companies around the world. The son of a country doctor, he recalls fond memories of small town third place experiences from his childhood. LaPorte is co-author with his wife, Carol, of *Life in the North Lane*, a locally popular book about living and working in Traverse City. They live on a cherry farm in Williamsburg, Michigan.

Barbara Mattingly is a native of New Orleans and has been a flight attendant for thirty years. She has always associated with groups of diverse people, of which the Neutral Ground Coffeehouse has been a generous supplier. She lives in Harahan, Louisiana.

Brian Mier is a journalist and has a master's degree in urban sociology. He served with co-contributor Steve Balkin on the board of directors of the Maxwell Street Historic Preservation Coalition. Raised on Chicago's north side, Meir currently lives in northeast Brazil, where he's found that there is no shortage of third places.

Richard Sexton is a noted photographer and writer on the topics of architecture, design, and the built environment. He is the author of *Vestiges of Grandeur: The Plantations of Louisiana's River Road* and *Parallel Utopias: The Quest for Community* and co-author of *New Orleans: Elegance and Decadence* and *In the Victorian Style*. His photographs have appeared in publications including *Harper's*, *Preservation*, and *Smithsonian*. He lives in New Orleans.

Ron Sher is the managing partner of a real estate development and management firm that specializes in the redevelopment of retail properties. Always interested in what makes communities work, Sher has recently created the Third Place Company, which is devoted to creating retail places that foster a sense of community and transform neighborhoods for the better.

James F. Smith, Ph.D., is a clinical psychologist and management consultant based in Atlanta, Georgia. His consulting focuses on the evaluation and development of exercise centers.

Steve Spracklen opened the Good Neighbor Coffee House with his wife Tracey in 1996. They live with their two daughters in Pensacola, Florida.

Denis Wood, a widely published geographer, taught at the School of Design at North Carolina State University for more than twenty years. He lives in Raleigh, North Carolina.